Erin Hung

Paper Parties

PAVILION

Contents

To my Papa in Heaven, who has taught me to celebrate

Introduction

My love affair with paper runs deep; the sight and scent of multiple shelves of neatly stacked paper stock in lots of different textures and weights sets my heart pounding at the possibilities of what I can create out of it. This love of paper, which began when I was a young girl with a pot of glue and lots of glitter, has grown into a fully fledged career in celebration stationery and gifts. Even now as I head up the BerinMade brand, which has products and reach spanning continents, it's important each day to remember where it all started; in my heart a small spark of creativity, materials that inspire me, and a huge dose of imagination.

There's a very strong case to be made for paper as a craft material; it's versatile, accessible and in most cases inexpensive. There's also something about its tangible nature that enables paper to spread joy from gifter to recipient in a very personal way. That's why we send cards for birthdays and wedding invitations – in fact the first wedding anniversary is marked with the gift of paper. Now more than ever, even in our highly digitized world, paper as a medium carries potent meaning as something that is momentous, heartfelt and, in the case of crafting, one of a kind.

To me, the point of crafting is to bring joy to our surroundings and our loved ones; half the fun is in creating something with your hands, and the other half is in seeing the delighted face of the person who is enjoying your creation. In our busy lives, it's so important to slow down, channel our creativity and show appreciation for those we love. If you're unsure about your crafting abilities, you'll find explanations of some of the basic skills on page 65. You can then dip your toes in the water by starting with some fun but simple craft projects such as You Float My Boat Place Names (page 82) and Sprinkles Confetti Balloons (page 140). I guarantee you'll come back and dive in for more.

To inspire you, the Lookbook at the front of the book showcases the finished projects in their party and everyday habitats. Hopefully, this will encourage you to throw your own parties, celebrate milestones and, even on ordinary days, show appreciation for those you love. Each Lookbook project cross-refers to the Tutorials chapter where you will find step-by-step instructions explaining how to make it, so feel free to jump to the instructions and start creating your own version whenever you like.

Each project tutorial is marked with a skill level ranging from 1 to 5; use this to help you choose a quick and easy project (level 1) for an afternoon of crafting, or go for a more complex project (level 5) that may take a weekend to complete. If you are looking for a specific type of project, such as gift wrap or party decorations, refer to the tutorials list (page 58). Once you have developed your papercrafting skills, you will be able to adapt and style each project to your heart's content. As a bonus, I have given you a peek into my little black book of favourite party suppliers (page 190).

Whether you are a novice crafter or a seasoned party planner, I hope that you will find plenty within the pages of this book to inspire you to create beautiful memories of your own. So go ahead and get your craft on, and don't forget to connect with me using @berinmade on Instagram and Twitter – I'd love to see what you make!

Lookbook

Pretty in Pink

This section is a homage to one of my first loves: the colour pink. When you are a little girl, you can unashamedly dress head-to-toe in it. Now that I have a little girl of my own, we love to play dressing up games and inevitably we end up in pink.

Especially in the sweet shades of pink, there is a risk of conjuring up images of Barbie's dream house and sugary-pink ballet tutus, which may be nice for the very young but could be a little too much for adult eyes. For a more sophisticated take on pink, you need to choose your shades wisely. When styling a pink-on-pink party, for example, go for pinks tinted with grey or beige (such as a dusty pink or nude pink). For brand inspirations, I look to high-fashion labels such as Miu Miu and Chloé – ultra-feminine but also fresh and modern. To keep things interesting, mix in a metallic such as copper or break up the look with some black and white pattern.

Oversized Sweets Wrap

One of the easiest ways to bring a whimsical touch to any creative idea is to play with scale. This is a fun way to add a little (or a lot of) sweetness to a gift. The pink and copper stripes add a touch of old-school charm. Pictured, page 9.

Tutorial: page 68

Doughnuts (About You) Toppers

Ah, doughnuts. These unsung heroes of confectionery are down-to-earth, yummy and comfortingly familiar – but stick a topper on them and they will be pretty much as fancy as their French cousins, macarons (not to mention a lot cuter). You can win me over with a doughnut stack sporting a heart-and-arrow topper any day.

Tutorial: page 78

Shake the Confetti Gift Wrap

Add a dash of fun in your gift wrap. This easy wrapping idea makes an impressive-looking present using just cellophane and coloured paper. For super-quick confetti, empty the contents of your hole punch tray.

Tutorial: page 70

Gift Wrap Tassels

For the finishing touch to a beautiful gift wrap, try a pair of pretty tassels. Leftover scraps of card made into classic gift tassels turn an ordinary ribbon tie into something special.

Tutorial: page 72

Secret Love Messages

Send a message from your heart! Hide your secret messages in this origami heart that doubles as an envelope or gift topper.

Tutorial: page 74

Take a Bow Cards

It's no secret that I love a good pun (that's how my husband Ben won me over, but that's a story for another time). These preppy beauties take only a few minutes to put together and give you extra cute points for any congratulatory – or other – messages inside.

Tutorial: page 76

Beside the Seaside

What inspires me most about the seaside is the richness of the textures you can find there: sandy beaches, smooth pebbles, the ridges on seashells and the foam of the waves breaking on the shore. When I close my eyes and think of the seaside, I can almost hear the waves crashing and feel the sand beneath my feet; I can picture the turquoise sea and feel the warmth of the sun on my face.

In this section I wanted to bring the experience of the seaside into the party setting by using a range of materials and textures: oil pastels, watercolours, Italian crêpe paper and even some jute string on card. Don't be afraid to combine natural, collected materials with paper – they contribute to the theme of natural textures.

You Float My Boat Place Names

Mussel shells have a beautiful iridescent colour like the deep, dark sea. Collect the shells at the seaside or save them next time you have moules-frites. Glue paper sails on to half shells to make instant boats and use them as place names or in a cluster as a table decoration.

Tutorial: page 82

Ahoy Flag Stirrers

Who can say no to cute little flags? These simple stirrers add a lovely finishing touch to seaside cocktails, and you can write little messages or your intials on them to make them extra-special.

Tutorial: page 86

Tie the Knot Announcements

Make your wedding announcement with clever knots, giving your guests an expectation of a beautiful day. I love the way the jute string gives so much tactility to the cards. Pictured, page 15.

Tutorial: page 80

Seafoam Chairback

This chairback has a sculptural look, while the movement in the crêpe paper also mimics the waves of the sea. Its all-white softness catches the light for an ultra-romantic feel. Make a special pair for a bridal couple, or place one on the table as a focal point.

Tutorial: page 84

Ice Cream Cone Messages

Such a sweet little project! Make one to give to someone special, or a whole batch as a party display. For a cheerful take on this, use coloured tissue for the pompoms.

Tutorial: page 90

Watercolour Gift Wrap

Inspired by the changing colours of the sea, this watercolour gift wrap can be made in batches and stored away for whenever you need it. If you don't have watercolour paints to hand, you can use poster paints or even diluted food colouring.

Tutorial: page 88

To the Moon and Back

Has anyone ever made you feel so elated that it sends you to the moon and back? If you know the feeling, you'll need to tell them so. This section includes an unexpected, playful twist on traditional love messages that feels a little cooler and more tongue-in-cheek.

There's always something romantic about looking up at a sky full of stars, but how do you make the extraterrestrial pretty on paper? By adding lots of silver glitter, of course. If you enjoy a feminine take on darker colours, this section is for you. I particularly love the star references, and the Comet Balloon Tassels (page 22) are my absolute favourite. This festive theme is testament to the fact that dark colours, too, can get their party on.

Frosty Snowflake Gift Toppers

Remember those fold-and-cut snowflakes you used to make at Christmas as a child? They are now coming back as gift toppers and are as pretty as ever. You can also scatter them on the table to decorate any winter celebrations.

Tutorial: page 98

Twinkling Stars Advent Calendar

I love a cute advent calendar idea. My version of an astro-themed advent is created with 24 mini-star boxes, either displayed on a wall or hung on the Christmas tree. Turn up the colours for a more traditional festive feel, or stick to sleek marble and silver for a contemporary look.

Tutorial: page 100

Astronaut Messages on a Starry Backdrop

Create an interactive 'guest book' with your own rockets (pictured, page 21). Ask your guests to fill them with messages and then send them off into space on a star-filled painted backdrop. Not only will you have a superb display at the party, you will also receive individual missives from your guests.

Tutorials: pages 92 & 96

Comet Balloon Tassels

There is something about a really good tassel that makes me feel all festive and ready to party. These tassels are great fun when the balloons are filled with helium and the tassels catch the wind.

Tutorial: page 102

I Lassoed the Moon for You Cupcake Box

I love thinking outside the box, and this hexagonal cupcake box does just that. Its clear top makes it perfect for showing off pretty things inside.

Tutorial: page 104

You're a Star Cards

I remember how gold star stickers at school made me beam with pride. Just because we are grown-ups, why should we stop giving stars to the people we appreciate?

Tutorial: page 94

Floral Fiesta

For me, a party without flowers is not a party at all. This section is dedicated to floral crafts and will appeal to anyone who cannot live without flowers, like me. I have used the warm colour palette of a Mexican fiesta, but you could choose a simpler, quieter palette for a softer and more romantic feel.

Flowers are a big part of my life and I love to see them on a daily basis. That's why most of the projects in this section can be made for everyday home décor as well as for special occasions. While flower-making does take patience, remember that the results are well worth it. Once you learn the basic skills of making petals, flower centres and stems (pages 106–111), you will be able to add flowers to all sorts of craft projects. My inability to keep a pot plant alive means that paper flowers will always be a welcome staple in my home.

Floral Letter

Decorated entirely with paper flowers, this floral letter packs a punch. I love this as party decor or as an eye-catching cake topper. You could also make a floral number and use it for a birthday or a first wedding anniversary.

Tutorial: page 112

Flower Power Party Poppers

Party poppers are typically found at New Year's Eve parties, but dressing them as flowers certainly gives them a summery look. Oh-so-pretty in bright colours, these poppers double as party decorations and are great fun for guests to pop at festive moments.

Tutorial: page 114

Frida Kahlo Flower Crown

I love floral crowns, but fresh ones can be expensive and only last a few days. This paper version combines all the basic flower-making techniques to create something with a real wow factor. Top tip: make them with your bridesmaids as a fun hen activity and they can wear their own creations at your wedding.

Tutorial: page 116

Floral Bomb Piñata

This floral bomb is such a showstopper that you might not want to break it open for the goodies inside. Hang it as a stunning party decoration and fill the interior with treats, ready for action. Your guests will love the sweet surprises.

Tutorial: page 118

Wrapping Paper Origami Lantern

Add lots of style to your party setting with a dash of impressive origami. The lantern can be made big or small, as you wish. A cluster of them is perfect hung from the ceiling or arranged on the floor.

Tutorial: page 122

Giant Flower Décor

These giant flowers have an irresistible charm and are a lovely way to decorate a room. They can be tacked to the wall or suspended on fishing wire from the ceiling. Their giant size means they will quickly transform any room, even on a tight budget. Plus, little girls love them. Pictured, page 27.

Tutorial: page 120

Wintry Forest

As the cold months approach, I look towards texture for warmth and comfort: sheepskin rugs, cashmere jumpers, the warm froth on my cappuccino – these keep me going when the days turn darker. This section is inspired by organic forms and materials, overlaid with a Scandi-style aesthetic. I love it that this party setting is laidback, modern and free of clutter.

To achieve the look, hold back on bright colours and choose shades found in nature. Also, consider the texture of the paper materials you buy – for example, would shimmering silver glitter paper or shiny silver foil work best for your project? To heighten interest and tactility, why not use both? All-white craft projects eliminate the distraction of colour and focus the eye on form and texture, so look for pretty doilies and tissue paper in different shades of white. This stylish but fun look is a great way to hone skills and gain confidence in creating a more pared-down, sophisticated party theme.

Snowball Lantern

This pretty project is sure to impress. Use a coloured paper lantern as the base, so that you get a lovely pop of colour when it is lit up. The lantern will look equally stunning indoors over a table or suspended from a tree branch for a garden party.

Tutorial: page 130

Doily Garlands

A simpler, quicker variation of the Snowball Lantern, these garlands are so darling and swoon-worthy. Although they are inspired by winter, the feminine edging on the doilies and their wispy feel would make them perfect for wedding decorations at any time of year.

Tutorial: page 132

Tassel Christmas Crackers

Homemade Christmas crackers are a real hit with guests of all ages. Fill them with sweets, confetti and your best (or worst) jokes, or with personalized Christmas messages and little gifts.

Tutorial: page 128

Foliage Wreath

This winter wreath can be whipped up on a cold Sunday afternoon. Made from a simple wooden hoop decorated with white and brown Kraft paper foliage, this half-filled wreath looks modern and minimalistic. Pictured, page 33.

Tutorial: page 124

Warm Your Heart Teabags

A cuppa that makes you smile is something worth having up your sleeve for winter mornings. Cut heart-shaped tabs and glue them onto the end of the teabag string while waiting for the kettle to boil. They are guaranteed to cheer up the worst morning grumpy-head.

Tutorial: page 134

Snowy Gift Wrap with Twig and Tassel Gift Topper

When I'm too short of time to go elsewhere, I sometimes struggle to find non-tacky wrapping paper on the high street. Then I remember that I can make my own. The snowy decoration turns plain brown paper into a work of art with just a few added paint spatters – a great project to do with children. The topper marries my love of geometric shapes and organic forms. The 'twig' is made from wire wrapped with jute string, but you could use a found twig from your back garden instead. Leave it bare and beautiful or spray it white for a clean, modern look before adding tags and tassels.

Tutorial: page 126

Goody Gumdrops

Big alert, sweet-tooths! If any party theme is sure to bring a beaming smile to your face, then this is it. Inspired by all the colours of the rainbow, this section brings a dash of innocence in its sugary, happy palette. You can base your party setting around the colours of your favourite retro sweet, or just go wild with any colours that you love.

All of the projects are simple to make, and the materials are not too precious for kids to have a go. Brightly coloured materials are easy to find on any high street. Love the look of neon? Then search for office supplies such as sticky notes and colour labels. Washi tapes and coloured card can be found in an array of colours, so pick and mix to your heart's content. Then play your favourite party mix, because there is a sugar rush to be danced off!

Sticky Notes Wall

This wall decoration really is a no-brainer; it's so easy to make that little ones could join in. I have used colour blocking for this background so that it does not steal focus, but you could also make a feature wall by building a pattern such as stripes or checks. Pictured, page 39.

Tutorial: page 138

Sparkling Candles Birthday Cards

These birthday cards combine two of my favourite things: neon tape and gold glitter. The birthday girl or boy will have candles that sparkle always. Top tip: for children, you can match the number of candles to the birthday age as a thoughtful memento.

Tutorial: page 142

I Want to Liquorice You Chair Streamers

Whenever I wander down the sweets aisle in a shop, liquorice allsorts seem to catch my eye because of their striking colour palette. These chair streamers are inspired by traditional folded paper chains and look lovely in a row.

Tutorial: page 136

Sprinkles Confetti Balloons

Confetti balloons are having a real moment in the party world. Make your own with just a clear balloon and some hand-cut tissue confetti. Leave the balloons loose to be kicked around or fill them with helium so they line the ceiling. These ones are inspired by rainbow-coloured confectionery sprinkles and bring a dash of whimsy to the cake table.

Tutorial: page 140

Ice Lolly Party Invitations

When I was a kid, my mum and I used to make ice lollies out of fresh fruit juice in the summer, and I remember opening the freezer every five minutes to check whether they had frozen. They were the best treats whenever my friends came around. These fun ice lolly invites are perfect for batch-making, and for those family-friendly summer parties.

Tutorial: page 144

Pastel Dreams

I'm a real colour-lover, but I think a palette of pastel shades is both timeless and beautiful when done well. The lightness of pastels gives them a feminine appeal, so they are perfect for baby showers, bridal showers and weddings. A word of warning, though: be careful what you pair your pastel palette with – because of its softness, it tends to become 'twee' when matched with shabby-chic lace or small-scale florals, so steer clear of these if you want to keep your theme modern.

For a contemporary take on this palette, combine it with geometric shapes and throw in a fun, unexpected element such as iridescent paper. I was inspired by the beautiful shapes of faceted gemstones and the natural patterns of agates and geodes; the different forms of these materials are fascinating and show off pastel shades perfectly.

You Are a Gem Cards

We are all gems, and I think everyone loves to hear it once in a while. These mini cards work as casual thank you notes and you can also make a folded version for more formal occasions such as an engagement, to say 'congrats' to your friend on her beautiful sparkler.

Tutorial: page 146

Iridescent Geometric Bowls

These on-trend geometric bowls look so good it's hard to believe they take only a few minutes to make, and as they are held together by modular origami techniques you don't even need glue or tape. They are the perfect handmade touches for last-minute parties and gatherings.

Tutorial: page 148

Mermaid Scales Backdrop

Inspired by the scales on a mermaid's tail, this wall decoration is all about harmonious colours so it works really well as a background. Choose two pastel colours (either cool blues, mauves and greens or warm oranges and yellows, not a contrast), and throw in shiny foil or pearlescent paper to get the iridescent effect. Pictured, page 43.

Tutorial: page 156

You Rock Place Names

I always love to play with scale. This means making things in miniature or oversized, like these 3D gems. They are a fantastic way to indicate seating, and guests can keep them to hang up. Who wouldn't love a big shiny rock to take home?

Tutorial: page 154

Painted Agate Slices

Agate slices catch the light and seem to change colour at different angles. These shimmering painted versions are sprinkled with glitter. They are most eye-catching when grouped together, so arrange them under a clear charger for a pretty place setting or attach them to stirrers for a tray of drinks.

Tutorial: page 152

All Kinds of Confetti

What is a party without confetti? The lightweight kind is perfect for showering someone and is easiest to photograph; heavier metallic confetti will fall faster and is great for table decorations.

Tutorial: page 150

Parisian Perfection

Oh, Paris! Where do I start about this wonderful city of love? Paris holds so much special meaning for me and my husband Ben – it's where we spent hours scouring antique markets after we first married, where we discovered many amazing cafés and bistros off the beaten track, and where we sampled pastries, crêpes and hot chocolate in the winter. Recently we visited for the first time since having our daughter Phoebe (who is now two years old) and experienced a very different Paris through her eyes – one that is sunnier, sweeter, more colourful; full of pink meringues, macarons and picnics in the park.

For this party theme I picked a lip print motif that is pretty and not too sultry, and matched it with a small dose of hand-painted Breton stripes and flashes of hot pink. Throw in plenty of pastries and sweets and you have an ultra-chic Parisian party.

Pop-up Lips Tent Cards

These clever pop-up cards can be used as dessert labels or place names. All you need to make them is a bit of white card and your favourite lipstick colour.

Tutorial: page 166

Dotty Macaron Box

I am not a baker and probably never will be, but jazzing up store-bought pastries and confectionery is a speciality of mine. I have this trick up my sleeve for when I don't have a whole lot of time, but still want to make things look extra-special.

Tutorial: page 168

Chic Personal Stationery

Send kisses, literally. Make your own collection of personalized mini cards, ready to use whenever you need them. And the best thing? You already have the main tool you'll need.

Tutorial: page 162

Baguette Wrappers

These baguette wrappers quickly jazz up plain bread rolls. Here they are displayed in a welcome basket, but you could also put one on each place setting with a personal note or a menu tucked in.

Tutorial: page 164

Pop the Bubbly Thank You Cards and Easy Liners

For the most festive thank you notes, send champagne-shaped notecards. The combination here of gold glitter and black card makes a chic statement. Write your note on the reverse, or attach a small magnet to make a keepsake. A hot pink envelope liner adds pizzazz to your post.

Tutorials: pages 158 & 160

Retro Festival

The relaxed, bohemian vibe and the beautiful earthy, muted colour palette are what I love most about this look. Festivals are vibrant hubs of music, food, culture and outdoor hang-outs, so it's nice to translate some of these features into party elements that channel a retro look.

Hunt for pretty floral prints in apricot, mustard yellows and textured browns, and add a little dash of gold glitter for a glam festive feel. Use wooden cutlery, crates and more organic elements to decorate the setting and tie all the colours together. Don't forget to add plenty of finger foods to share!

Floral Print
Food Cones

Perfect for lovers of finger-food, these lovely cones can hold dainty waffles, churros or even ice-cream cones.

Tutorial: page 170

Retro Print Cutlery Holders

Not only can these holders house cutlery, there is also a little pocket for condiments. Write your guests' names on the brown Kraft paper insert so they can double up as place names for a sit-down dinner.

Tutorial: page 172

Glitter-dipped Paper Feathers

These striking paper feathers look pretty in colourful drinks as stirrers. Alternatively, bigger versions can be used to make an eye-catching garland (pictured, page 53). Their shimmery surface glistens in the light and they look oh-so-fabulous on a sunny summer's day.

Tutorial: page 174

Oops-a-Daisy Chain Choker

Make a daisy chain choker that won't wilt. A beautiful alternative to a floral crown, this choker is quieter and more subtle, perfect for the understated flower-lover.

Tutorial: page 176

Cupcake Anemones

The anemone is a real winner, even with non-flower-loving types. Their striking dark centres make them stand out from the crowd, and their non-fussy shape keeps their form clean and more gender-neutral. Now you can make them all year round!

Tutorial: page 178

Scallop-edged Stationery

Bring a dash of retro chic to your stationery with a glittered scallop edge. This edging technique is so versatile that it can be used across an entire set of stationery, from envelopes to cards and tags.

Tutorial: page 180

Tutorials

Papercraft Materials

Online shopping is an amazing resource for buying craft materials, and sometimes the selection surpasses what you can find in a local art and craft store. The search functions on sites such as Amazon or eBay allow you to do a one-stop craft shop, sourcing materials from multiple suppliers to be delivered to your doorstep. Nearly all of the materials used in this book can be sourced online, and you will find a list of my favourite suppliers on page 191. Here are some of the papers and materials to look for.

Coloured papers and cards

are the staple materials in any papercrafting kit. These come in different weights, measured in gsm (grams per square metre). Generally, 80–150 gsm is considered paper weight, which is great for origami folding and making paper cutouts, envelopes and liners. Weights of 200–250 gsm are classified as light card or heavy paper, and are used for more structured projects such as Christmas crackers and some paper flowers. Weights above that are considered card. Card weights are generally used for greeting cards, stationery, invitations and crafts that require more durability, such as cake toppers.

Confetti

can be used to enhance your craft projects. Buy it from party supply stores or make your own (see page 150).

Rolled papers

include crêpe paper, Italian crêpe (sometimes called florist crêpe) and tissue paper. These fragile papers are often sold in rolls for ease of transit. Large sheets of wrapping paper and cellophane are also sold in rolls.

Paper supplies

for the office and kitchen such as coloured tape, sticky notes, cupcake holders, doilies and coffee filters can all be repurposed for crafting because of their bright colours and ready-made shapes. Next time you visit an office supplies store or even the stationery section in a supermarket, pay attention to the goodies you can find there.

Lightweight papers

such as tissue paper (which can be sold folded or rolled) as well as crêpe streamers are generally used for decorative and more fragile crafts such as pompoms, tassels and streamers, or as packaging padding.

Specialist papers

designed for crafting purposes include glitter paper, mirror card, iridescent card, mylar card, contact paper, woodgrain-textured paper, marbled paper and foamboard. I pick them up when I come across them and store them for special occasions or times when inspiration hits. Specialist papers are normally sold as flat sheets in A sizes. For more information about paper sizes, see page 189.

Tools and Supplies

Most of the tools shown here are things you will probably already have in your home, though you may need to buy a few specialist items. You will also require a selection of functional supplies such as glue and double-sided tape (categorized as 'tools' in the tutorials), as well as decorative supplies including paint, ribbon and string.

Cutting and scoring tools

These include rulers, bone scorers, scalpels, scissors, fringing scissors, hole punches, punches of various shapes and wire cutters. Scissors will be the most frequently used tool in your craft kit, but if you take good care of them they can last for years. To extend their lifetime, designate scissors for specific materials, such as sticky materials and tape, ribbon and fabric, and paper and card.

Securing and fixing tools

Including floral wire, string, masking tape, fishing wire, double-sided tape, washi tape and ribbon.

Painting and decorating tools

You will need paintbrushes and old brushes reserved for applying glue. Flat brushes are useful for painting larger surfaces. I generally use water-based paints such as gouache, watercolour and acrylic for papercrafts, because unprimed paper and card will not take oil-based paints well. Gouache and acrylic will give greater coverage, while watercolour is softer and allows the background to show through.

Glue

Glueing is generally done with PVA glue (a water-based paper glue), all-purpose glue (a stronger glue for cards and other materials or glue stick (for lighter-weight papers). A hot glue gun works well for glitter paper.

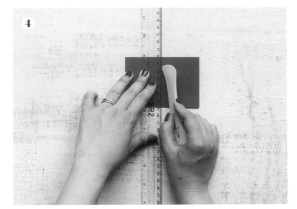

Core Skills

The following techniques are used multiple times in the projects. Also included here are instructions for making a basic tassel and pompom (two of my favourite things), which you can make on their own for decoration or as part of more advanced projects.

1. Cutting from templates

Photocopy the required template and overlay the printed template on the paper or card that needs to be cut. If the template is a simple shape, just hold the two pieces together and cut out with scissors. If the shape is more complicated, first cut out the template then lay it on the paper and draw a pencil outline around it. Remove the template and cut the paper along the drawn line. You can use a scalpel for cutting more intricate shapes.

2. Folding pleats

Pleats are a series of opposing folds (which is to say folds in opposite directions). To fold even pleats, crease the paper by folding it in half and then open it out flat again. Crease again by folding each half into further halves, using the previous crease as a guide and always creasing the paper in the same direction. Continue creasing the paper in this way. The more you crease, the smaller the increments become. When you are satisfied with the increments between creases, open the paper flat and then start folding the paper in opposing folds, again using the creases as guides.

3. Fringing with a scalpel or everyday scissors

Cutting with a scalpel or normal scissors lets you set the increments of the fringe, but is a slower method compared to fringing scissors. For best results, cut the fringing with a scalpel using a ruler as a guide. Protect your work surface with an old magazine or a cutting mat.

4 & 5. Scoring and folding

To score means to slightly indent the surface of the paper without piercing through to the other side. Scoring is used in preparation for any folding that needs to be clean and accurate. The break in the paper acts as a guide for the fold, and this is especially important when folding cards so that the surface of the paper doesn't break when it's folded, and gives a neater, more professional finish. Scoring is usually done with a bone scorer, but you can use the blunt side of a scalpel or the pointed tip of a compass. To score, simply align your ruler where you want to fold, and run the scorer (or the pointy instrument, lightly) along the edge. You may want to line your work surface with an old magazine or a cutting mat for best results and to protect the surface.

6. Fringing with fringing scissors

This is the quickest way to create a lot of fringes, so it is great for piñatas and for making confetti. Fringing scissors have multiple blades that cut into the paper simultaneously so that you can fringe sections at a time. However, because the increments of the blades are set, you cannot alter the width of the fringes.

Making tassels

1 To make a basic tassel, cut a stack of 4–5 rectangular pieces of tissue paper; the paper should be twice the length of tassel required and wide enough to give the desired fullness of tassel. Fringe each side of the paper lengthways, leaving the centre uncut as this will form the top of the tassel.

2 Roughly pleat and gather the centre of the tissue.

3 Twist the centre of the paper like gently wringing a towel, then fold the twisted centre to form a loop. Secure the loop with string, ribbon or a strip of paper glued around it.

Making pompoms

1 To make a basic pompom, cut a stack of 4–5 rectangular pieces of tissue paper; the size of the rectangles will depend upon the size of pompom you wish to make. Evenly pleat the paper stack (see pages 64–65) and then fold it into a closed accordion. Trim both ends into rounded shapes.

2 Secure the centre tightly with ribbon, string or a rubber band. Fan out both ends of the paper accordion.

3 Carefully separate the layers of tissue and fluff into a pompom shape.

Oversized
Sweets Wrap

2

5

4

DIFFICULTY
✁ ✁ ✁ ✁ ✁

MATERIALS
Wraps 1 large gift
› Pink tissue paper
  (large enough
  to wrap present,
  doubled up)
› Pink/white baker's
  twine (20cm/8in)
› Copper card (for
  metallic stripes)
› Pink emulsion paint,
  small sample pot
  (for painted stripes)

TOOLS
› Scissors
› Double-sided tape
› Scalpel, ruler and
  cutting mat (for
  metallic stripes)
› Wide masking tape
  and flat paintbrush
  (for painted stripes)

Not only is this wrapping idea quick and easy to do, it also transforms the gift into a display item that guarantees it a spot as the most charming present in the pile at any party. I use it a lot, especially for circular boxes that can be fiddly to wrap.

1 Measure out and cut a double layer of tissue paper, allowing for an overhang at each end of the present. Wrap the present and secure the centre overlap of the paper with double-sided tape. Repeat with another layer for added opacity if necessary, especially if the gift box is a darker colour than the tissue.

2 Bunch up the tissue paper at each end and twist it tightly, close to the gift box. Be careful not to pull too hard because the tissue could break on any box corners.

3 Secure each end with twine tied in a double knot, then trim off the tails of the knots.

4 To add metallic stripes, use a scalpel and ruler to cut strips of card about 3cm (1¼in) wide and long enough to wrap around the present. Cut as many as needed, then line them up on the present. When you are happy with the spacing, wrap them around the gift and tape down securely with double-sided tape.

5 To add painted stripes, apply strips of masking tape around the present. Use a flat brush to paint over the masking tape.

Shake the Confetti
Gift Wrap

MATERIALS
To wrap 1 gift
› Pink gift wrap
› Pink and nude-coloured tissue paper (1 sheet each, A1 size)
› Copper metallic paper (1 sheet, A5 size)
› Cellophane

TOOLS
› Scissors
› Double-sided tape
› Clear tape

I love things that are interactive, and this is possibly one of the easiest wraps to do because it does not require any new skills. It is also a lovely wrapping idea for sending a gift by post because the confetti adds an element of surprise when the package is opened.

1 Cut the gift wrap to size, wrap the gift and secure with double-sided tape.

2 Cut long strips, about 5mm (¼in) wide, of pink and nude tissue paper and copper paper. Cut the strips into small pieces, about 1.5cm (⅝in) long, to make confetti.

3 Cut a piece of cellophane large enough to fit around the gift, then sprinkle confetti onto the centre of the cellophane. Place the gift top downwards on the sprinkled confetti.

4 Sprinkle more confetti around the sides, then wrap the cellophane around the gift like normal gift wrap. Secure with clear tape. If necessary, push more confetti between the gift wrap and cellophane before sealing the last open end.

Gift Wrap
Tassels

2

4

5

3

6

DIFFICULTY

✂ ✂ ✂ ✂ ✂

MATERIALS

To make 1 set of tassels

› Pink ribbon (1cm/⅜in wide)
› 1 sheet each of copper and pink paper (A5 size)

TOOLS

› Scissors
› Fast-drying PVA glue
› Fringing scissors (optional)

Tassels are one of those embellishments that never go out of style. These tassels are so understated that they can be paired with a busy pattern; try combining them with Shake the Confetti Gift Wrap (see page 70). With just a ribbon, some scraps of card and scissors, you're good to go.

1 Measure and cut the ribbon so that it can be tied around the gift with a knot, leaving 3–4cm (1¼–1½in) excess at the ends.

2 At one end, fold the left edge (about a third of the width of the ribbon) over the centre third and glue in place. Repeat with the right edge, then do the same at the other end of the ribbon. This makes the ends narrower to fit inside the tassel.

3 Cut two 20 x 2cm (8 x ¾in) strips of copper or pink paper for the tassel fringing. Then cut two narrow 5cm (2in) strips of the other colour paper to bind the top of the tassel.

4 Use fringing scissors or normal scissors to fringe the longer strips widthways, cutting about three-quarters of the way through.

5 Apply a line of glue along the uncut edge of the first fringed strip, then wrap it around one end of the ribbon.

6 Glue one of the small strips of paper around the top of the tassel. Repeat to add a tassel to the other end of the ribbon.

These traditional origami hearts are oldies but goodies. For best results, use lightweight paper of about 80–100 gsm to get clean folding lines – printer paper works well if you have nothing else to hand. An A4 sheet makes four mini hearts (I love mini things), but if you need the heart to be bigger, just skip step 3 below.

1 Place the paper in front of you with the long edges horizontal. Fold down the top right corner so that the right edge aligns with the bottom edge of the sheet and make a crease. Cut off the rectangle exposed along the left edge and discard. Unfold the paper; it should be a perfect square.

2 Fold the paper into four equal squares and then cut them out.

3 Place the first square in front of you, white side up if the paper is single-sided. Referring to the guide on page 188, fold in half vertically, make a crease and then unfold. Repeat horizontally.

4 Fold the bottom edge up to the horizontal crease and then turn the model over.

5 Fold the bottom left corner up to the centre vertical crease, aligning the bottom edge with the centre crease. Repeat on the right side and then turn the model over.

6 Fold the left and right edges in so that they align with the vertical crease.

7 Fold the top two corners down, aligning the top edge with the centre of the model on each side.

8 Fold the top tip down to align with the bottom tip, then open and flatten the two 'pockets' that are created.

9 Insert the tip of the top layer into the pocket on the layer below.

10 Fold down the top left and right corners, then fold down the two top points.

11 Repeat steps 4–11 with the three remaining pink squares.

12 Write on small scraps of paper and slip a secret message into each heart.

Take a
Bow Cards

1

2

4

DIFFICULTY

✂ ✂ ✂ ✂ ✂

MATERIALS
To make 1 card
› Pink tissue paper
  (7 x 9cm/2¾ x 3½in)
› Copper glitter
› Pink card
  (10 x 20cm/4 x 8in)

TOOLS
› Scissors
› Double-sided tape
› Scorer
› Ruler
› PVA glue

This pretty bow is a really good basic embellishment that you can put on lots of things, such as presents or place cards. You could even string lots of them together to make a garland. Once you have mastered the technique of pleating paper, try using coloured card for a more structured look.

1 Fold the tissue paper lengthways into even pleats (see page 64), aiming for pleats about 5mm (¼in) deep. The finished piece should be a 7 x 0.5cm (2¾ x ¼in) pleated strip.

2 Cut a 2cm (¾in) piece of double-sided tape. Cover one side of the tape with copper glitter, leaving about 5mm (¼in) free at one short end. Tap off the excess glitter.

3 Pinch the centre of the pleated tissue together and wrap the glittered tape around it, securing the end onto the glitterless section of the tape.

4 Using a scorer and ruler, score and then fold the pink card in half. Glue the bow onto the centre.

Doughnuts (About You) Toppers

MATERIALS

To make 10 toppers
- › Cocktail sticks (10 sticks)
- › White paint
- › Pink paper (1 sheet, A5 size)
- › Double-sided copper metallic paper (1 sheet, A5 size)

TOOLS

- › Fine paintbrush
- › Scissors
- › Heart-shaped punch (optional)
- › PVA glue
- › Black brush pen

I love making things, but as a busy working mum I can't really find a spare hour on an ordinary day to bake a batch of doughnuts. However, I can find five minutes to make some toppers. Call me a cheat, but what I've found is that even if my doughnuts (or cupcakes, or pies) are not home-baked, I can jazz up store-bought baked goods to look lovely and personal. So that's pretty much the same, isn't it?

1 Paint each cocktail stick with white paint, leaving about 1.5cm (^{5}/$_8$in) unpainted at one end.

2 Using the templates (see page 182), cut out heart shapes from pink paper and arrow tails from copper paper (or use a heart-shaped punch for the hearts). You will need two of each shape per topper.

3 For each topper, cover one side of an arrow tail with glue. Place the painted end of a cocktail stick down the centre of the arrow tail. Place another arrow tail on top, pressing the two sides together to secure.

4 Use scissors to fringe each side of the arrow tail.

5 Cover one side of a heart with glue. Place the cocktail stick down the centre of the heart, positioning it so that 1cm (^{3}/$_8$in) of the unpainted end of the stick protrudes below the heart. Place another heart on top, pressing the two sides together to secure.

6 Use a black brush pen to add stripes on the cocktail stick between the heart and arrow tail.

✂ ✂ ✂ ✂ ✂

MATERIALS
To make 8 cards
› Jute string (1 roll)
› White card
  (1 sheet, A4 size)
› Yellow ochre
  gouache paint

TOOLS
› Scissors
› Fine paintbrush
› PVA glue and
  flat paintbrush

I will readily admit that these wedding announcements can be fiddly to make at first. The key to it is to start with the two 'fish' swimming in opposite directions, with the loop of each fish lying over or under the other's tail. I love a little challenge, so I find these oddly satisfying to make. Once you get the hang of them, they are actually a lot of fun.

1 Cut six 10cm (4in) lengths of string and separate into two sections, each with three pieces of string.

2 Referring to the guide on page 188, loop each section of string to form two 'fish' swimming towards each other. Overlap them so that one fish's head (the loop) is sitting on top of the cross-over point of the other fish's tail.

3 Copy the knot in the photograph by pulling the ends of the tails under or over the loops as shown.

4 Cut the card into eight rectangles, about 7.5 x 10 cm (3 x 4in) each. With the short edges of the card horizontal, paint the names of the couple near the bottom.

5 Write any personal messages to the recipient on the back of the card.

6 Secure the knot centrally on the front of the card with PVA glue, applying the glue sparingly on the tails. Hold down and allow to dry for 30 minutes, then trim off the excess string.

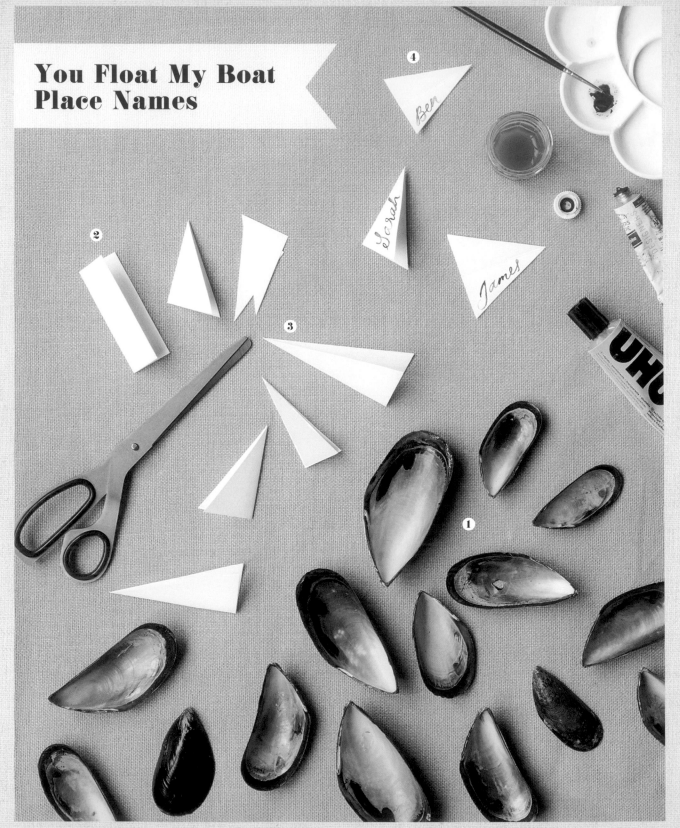

You Float My Boat Place Names

MATERIALS
To make 4 boats
- › Two mussel shells (opened)
- › White card (1 sheet, A6 size)
- › Blue gouache or watercolour paint

TOOLS
- › Scissors
- › Fine paintbrush
- › All-purpose glue

I love combining found materials with crafts, and nature's organic shapes are hard to beat. On a recent trip to the seaside, my daughter Phoebe and I collected lots of pebbles, shells and even coral at the beach, giving me exciting inspiration for new projects. However, you don't need to travel to the seaside to make these place names – just collect mussel shells after a meal or ask your local fishmonger.

1 Clean the mussel shells thoroughly in warm soapy water. Allow to dry overnight, then carefully snap open to separate into half shells.

2 Cut a small rectangular piece of card for each sail. To make the sail in proportion to the shell, the height and width of the card should equal the length and width of the mussel shell respectively.

3 Fold the card in half lengthways. With the fold on the left, cut from the bottom right corner up to the top left folded corner to make a triangular sail.

4 Paint the name of the guest on one side of the sail.

5 Attach the sail to the inside of the shell with a small blob of glue, holding the sail in place for half a minute until dry. Repeat for the other half shells.

MATERIALS

To make 1 chairback

› White Italian crêpe paper (1 roll)
› Metal wire (1 roll)
› Ribbon (60cm/ 24in long, 3mm/ ⅛in wide)

TOOLS

› Scissors
› Wire cutters

This chairback is made from ruffled layers of beautiful Italian crêpe paper, which has an incredible sculptural quality. Once you become acquainted with the material, you will be able to work wonders with it. The paper's bumpy ridges catch the light so that it photographs like a dream. This project has a high skill level rating because each layer takes patience and time to complete, but the results are well worthwhile.

1 Roll out a section of crêpe paper and observe the direction of the grain. You will see long thick ridges going in one direction, with the finer, more condensed grain running perpendicular to them.

2 Cut a strip of crêpe paper, about 40cm (16in) wide, with the thick ridges running along the length of the strip. The length of the crêpe should be equal to the width of the chair back.

3 Fold the paper in half lengthways and cut a piece of wire the same length as the paper. Using the wire tip to pierce the paper, 'sew' in and out through the folded edge about 3cm (1¼in) in from the fold.

4 When you reach the end, bend the end of the wire into a U-shaped loop so that the crêpe will not slide off.

5 Push the crêpe paper along the wire so that it has a slightly pleated effect like a curtain, then bend the other end of the wire into a loop (cut off any excess wire if necessary before forming the loop).

6 Using both hands, take small sections of the crêpe paper and lightly pull against the direction of the fine grain to sculpt. Repeat until the entire piece is sculpted into a ruffled layer.

7 Make several layers of ruffles of varying widths and arrange them into a shape you like.

8 Cut two 30cm (12in) lengths of ribbon. Thread one piece of ribbon through all the wire loops on one side of the ruffled layers and secure with a double knot. Repeat on the other side. Use the ribbons to tie the ruffled layers to the chair.

Ahoy Flag
Stirrers

2

5

4

MATERIALS

To make 10 stirrers
› Jute string (1 roll)
› Coffee stirrers
  (10 sticks)
› Light grey card

TOOLS

› Scissors
› Double-sided tape

If you are planning a party, this is a project that can benefit from a production chain (aka, a team of craft-loving friends) – one station to wrap the string, another to cut the flags and another to assemble. The stirrers are so straightforward and easy to make that you can just turn on some tunes and have a good natter while getting your craft on.

1 Cut about 10cm (4in) of jute string for each stirrer.

2 Leaving 4cm (1½in) of space at the top, wrap the string around a coffee stirrer and secure the two ends with a tight knot. Trim off the excess string.

3 Cut a 10 x 1cm (4 x ³⁄₈in) strip of card and line one side with double-sided tape, trimming the tape to fit if necessary. Peel off the protective layer.

4 Lay the strip of card flat and place the coffee stick centrally on top, as shown opposite, with the string and long end of the stirrer below the card. Fold the card onto itself so that the sticky sides come together.

5 Trim the end of the tag into a V-shaped swallowtail. Repeat steps 2–4 with the remaining stirrers.

Watercolour Gift Wrap

DIFFICULTY
✂ ✂ ✂ ✂ ✂

MATERIALS
To make 1 sheet
› White oil pastel
› White cartridge paper (no lighter than 120gsm)
› Blue and green watercolour paints

TOOLS
› Old newspaper or plastic
› Paint dish
› Flat paintbrush

This project uses a neat little trick that was a favourite of mine as a child. We called it magic painting, where we would use oil pastel to scribble an 'invisible' message onto white paper. The recipient then painted over the paper with watercolour to reveal the secret message. The oil pastel acts as a barrier between the watercolour and paper, so that the paper remains clear of paint where the oil pastel has been applied. Clever, huh?

1 Line your work area with old newspaper or plastic. Using white oil pastel, scribble a pattern on the paper, such as stripes or figures of eight.

2 Make a blue wash and green wash in the paint dish. The best way to do this is to start with a small blob of paint, then add water, mix and test on a scrap piece of paper. Repeat until you are satisfied with the depth of the colour.

3 Paint the entire paper, alternating sections of blue and green. Experiment with adding areas of more diluted or more concentrated paint for movement in the colour. Allow to dry overnight.

MATERIALS
To make 4 cones
› White card
  (1 sheet, A5 size)
› White tissue paper
  (4 sheets, A2 size)
› Ribbon (3mm/
  ⅛in wide)
› Brown card (1 sheet,
  A4 size)
› Brown gouache paint

TOOLS
› Scissors
› Hole punch
› Fine paintbrush
› Double-sided
  tape (optional)
› All-purpose glue

Pompoms are so versatile and can be integrated into many projects. The fluffy, pretty texture of the pompom makes the perfect paper version of an ice-cream cone. You can make multicoloured pompoms for a super fun vibe, or keep them white for a seaside theme. A message tag is tied to the pompom so that it doubles as a gift – after all, why send a card when you can send an ice-cream cone?

1 For each cone, cut a 2 x 6cm (¾ x 2½in) strip of white card for the message tag. Cut a V-shaped swallowtail at one end and hole punch the other end.

2 Make a pompom (see page 67), using 20 x 10cm (8 x 4in) pieces of white tissue paper and tying the centre with 30cm (12in) ribbon. Leave a long end of ribbon for attaching the pompom to the cone and a shorter end for the tag. Don't fully fluff out the pompom just yet.

3 Write a message on the tag, string it onto the shorter end of the ribbon and secure in place with a double knot. Now fluff out the pompom fully.

4 Using the template on page 186, cut out the cone shape from brown card. Paint a diagonal cross-hatch pattern on the card with brown gouache.

5 Once dry, roll the brown card into a cone shape. To secure the back, apply double-sided tape or glue, then hold tight.

6 Thread the long end of the pompom ribbon through the bottom of the cone.

7 With your index finger, push the centre of the pompom firmly into the cone, so that the pompom sits nicely lodged inside.

8 Tighten the ribbon through the bottom of the cone and secure with glue, holding the ribbon down onto the card until dry. Trim off the excess ribbon.

Starry
Backdrop

MATERIALS
To make 1 large piece
› Blue and white
  acrylic or
  gouache paint
› Cartridge paper (no
  lighter than 120 gsm)

TOOLS
› Old newspaper
  or plastic
› Paint dish
› Flat paintbrush
› Fine paintbrush
› Spare brush or pencil

This paper background works as a basic gift wrap, as well as a background or card – for example, Astronaut Messages (see page 96) and You're a Star Cards (see page 94). I really love the simplicity of the idea, but also the therapeutic feeling of putting a big flat paintbrush onto paper. Be sure to cover your work area – and get a little messy!

1 Line your work area with old newspaper or plastic. Make a blue wash in the paint dish. The best way to do this is to start with a small blob of paint, then add water, mix and test on a scrap piece of paper. Repeat until you are satisfied with the depth of colour.

2 Using a flat brush and rough strokes in different directions, paint the entire paper. Experiment with adding areas of more diluted or more concentrated paint for movement in the colour.

3 Slightly dilute some white paint until the consistency is drippy but still opaque (gouache is best for this). Dip a fine paintbrush in the paint and flick it towards the paper to add speckles of white. For more concentrated areas, tap the dipped brush against something such as a spare brush or pencil.

You're a
Star Cards

94

✂ ✂ ✂ ✂ ✂

MATERIALS
To make 1 card
› Starry Backdrop card (see page 92), trimmed to A5 size
› Silver glitter paper (1 sheet, A4 size)
› White paper (small scrap)
› Black envelope (C6 size)

TOOLS
› Scorer
› Ruler
› Pencil
› Scissors
› Fringing scissors (optional)
› Glue stick

I love any excuse to crack out my glitter paper, and these star cards absolutely fit the bill. Attach multiple stars to create a starscape, or opt for a single shooting star with a curly fringe.

1 Using a scorer and ruler, score the Starry Backdrop card in half widthways and fold into A6 size.

2 Mark out a five-pointed star on the reverse of the silver paper and cut it out. Repeat for as many stars as desired, varying the shape and size.

3 If making a shooting star, cut a strip of white paper half the width of the star and about 5cm (2in) long. Use fringing scissors or normal scissors to fringe the strip lengthways, cutting about three-quarters of the way.

4 Glue the uncut end of the fringed strip to the reverse of the shooting star. Trim the fringe to a length you are happy with.

5 Glue the star or stars onto the front of the card in a design you like.

Astronaut Messages

MATERIALS
To make 3 rockets
› Silver, black and white thin card (10 x 15cm/4 x 6in each)
› Navy tissue paper (3 pieces, 10 x 15cm/ 4 x 6in)
› Iridescent fringe (small amount)
› Silver glitter paper (1 sheet, A4 size)
› Silver string (3 pieces, 10cm/4in)
› Iridescent star confetti (optional)

TOOLS
› Scissors
› Fast-drying PVA glue
› Fringing scissors (optional)
› Hot glue gun
› Double-sided tape (optional)
› Scalpel and cutting mat

As a child I used to make rockets out of cardboard toilet roll tubes and plenty of glitter glue, so I guess not much has changed. This is an updated version, creating a 'guest book' where guests can leave little messages in the rockets. You can decorate the fringe with iridescent star confetti, as well as the iridescent fringe that is sometimes used as a packaging material.

1 Choose the colour of card to use for the body of the first rocket and place it in front of you, long edges horizontal. Apply PVA glue along the bottom edge and press a piece of tissue paper on it with an overlap of about 5mm (¼in).

2 Use fringing or normal scissors to fringe the overhanging tissue paper, cutting about three-quarters through.

3 Cut a few 10cm (4in) lengths of iridescent fringe and attach them individually to the top of the fringed tissue section with a dot of glue. Trim any overhanging ends of iridescent fringe, to align with the tissue fringe.

4 Wrap the card into a cylinder with the tissue hanging on the inside and secure with a line of hot glue or double-sided tape along one edge and an overlap of 5mm (¼in).

5 Cut a 5mm x 15cm (¼ x 6in) strip of silver glitter paper and attach it around the bottom of the cylinder with PVA glue.

6 Gather the tissue fringe together under the cylinder and tie into a bunch with silver string. Trim the ends of the string to about 2cm (¾in). Use a dot of hot glue to attach an iridescent star to each end. Use PVA glue to attach iridescent stars to some of the tissue fringing.

7 Using the template (see page 182), cut the rocket point out of silver glitter paper. Use a scalpel to cut out the slot for inserting messages.

8 Wrap the glitter paper into a conical shape that will fit onto the end of the cylinder. Secure with a line of hot glue along one edge and a small overlap. Apply hot glue or PVA around the top rim of the cylinder and attach the cone.

Frosty Snowflake Gift Toppers

DIFFICULTY

✂ ✂ ✂ ✂ ✂

MATERIALS

To make a handful of snowflakes

› Silver glitter paper or navy gift wrap
› White paper (1 sheet, A4 size)

TOOLS

› Masking tape
› Scalpel and cutting mat
› Ruler (optional)
› Double-sided tape

One of the biggest reasons to love papercuts (not the ouch kind!) is that they can be immensely therapeutic and satisfying. If you are anything like me and your life is always go-go-go, there is something about the art of slowing down that is oddly enjoyable. Make these snowflakes as toppers or pretty displays.

1   Wrap the gift with silver glitter paper or navy gift wrap.

2   Lay your chosen snowflake template (see page 182) on top of the white paper and secure in place with masking tape. Cut out the snowflake with a scalpel, using a ruler to help if necessary.

3   Use a little double-sided tape to secure the snowflakes to the top of the present.

Twinkling Stars Advent Calendar

DIFFICULTY

✂ ✂ ✂ ✂ ✂

MATERIALS
To make 24 stars
› Silver thin card
  (4 sheets, A4 size)
› Marble-patterned
  thin card (4 sheets,
  A4 size)
› White acrylic or
  gouache paint
› Sweets or small
  surprises (24 pieces)

TOOLS
› Scissors
› Scorer or scalpel
› Ruler
› PVA glue
› Fine paintbrush

I love, love, love these stars as an advent calendar. Let's face it, Christmas is a time when the appearance of bright, gaudy colours escalates rather quickly, so the minimalist shape and subtle shades of these stars are always a welcome break for me.

1 Using the template (see page 182), cut out 12 pieces in cards of each colour, so you have a total of 24 pieces.

2 Using a scorer or scalpel and a ruler, score the lines marked on the template. Crease along each scored line.

3 Fold the three tabs inwards and apply PVA glue to each, then fold the pentagon section on top and press down over the tabs to secure. There should still be one open edge.

4 Put a finger inside the pocket and encourage it into a three-dimensional shape. From the outside, push inwards between the points to form the star shape.

5 Paint the numbers 1–24 onto each of the stars, as shown opposite.

6 Fill each star with a sweet or other surprise, then close by pushing the open end inwards.

Comet Balloon Tassels

MATERIALS

To make 1 string of tassels

› White and navy tissue paper (5 sheets each, A2 size)
› Silver foil fringe curtain
› Silver string (150cm/5ft)
› White or black round balloon

TOOLS

› Scalpel and cutting mat
› Ruler
› Sticky tape

If one tassel is fun, then a whole string of them is lots of fun. This project includes tassels made from tissue paper and silver strands from a metallic fringe curtain all strung together. You can attach the string of tassels to a balloon or hang them horizontally as a garland – that's a win-win choice.

1 To make tissue paper tassels, place all five sheets of the same colour tissue paper together in a pile and fold in half lengthways, with the fold at the top and loose edges at the bottom.

2 Use a scalpel and ruler to fringe the bottom of the paper, spacing the cuts about 5mm (¼in) apart and leaving 3cm (1¼in) of paper uncut at the folded edge.

3 Cut the fringed strip into 5cm (2in) wide sections.

4 Unfold each section and roll the uncut paper in the middle to twist it together. Fold in half again to form a loop, then twist the loop tightly.

5 To make fringe curtain tassels, cut the fringe into 60cm (24in) lengths. Place about 30 lengths together in a pile and fold in half. Wrap a piece of sticky tape around the fringe, about 1cm (⅜in) from the fold.

6 Trim the ends of all the tassels to neaten.

7 Holding the string vertically in front of you, tie the tassels onto the string, alternating colours and overlapping the bottom half of the new tassel with the top half of the previous tassel each time, as shown opposite. Tie the string of tassels to the inflated balloon.

DIFFICULTY

✂ ✂ ✂ ✂ ✂

MATERIALS

To make 1 box
› Marble-patterned thin card (1 sheet, A3 size)
› Cellophane (6cm/2½in square)

TOOLS

› Scissors
› Scorer or scalpel
› Ruler
› Double-sided tape

During my middle school years growing up in the United States, we used to take cupcakes to school on our birthdays as a treat for our friends. During lesson breaks I would continually peek into the box to make sure that the icing was not dented, because let's face it, the icing is the best part. Cupcake icing is now fancier and more colourful than ever, so I love this box that lets you show off the goodies inside.

1 Using the templates (see page 183), cut out the pieces of the box from thin card.

2 Using a scorer or scalpel and a ruler, score the lines marked on the templates. Crease along each scored line.

3 Take the large base piece and, one by one, apply double-sided tape to each tab and attach it to the inside of the adjacent side section to create a three-dimensional hexagonal box base.

4 Do the same with the lid piece, taping each tab to the inside of the adjacent side section.

5 Apply small pieces of tape around the edge of the hexagonal hole on the inside of the lid. Stick the cellophane square over the hole.

Floral Basics

Floral crafts are really a category of their own, and there are entire books devoted to making paper flowers. Before starting any of the floral projects, familiarize yourself with these simple techniques for making the basic flower components. Once you master the materials and foundational skills of making flowers, you can adapt them to different palettes, papers and scales. The possibilities are endless.

MATERIALS
› Foil
› Green floral wire
› Flower-coloured and green Italian crêpe paper

TOOLS
› Hot glue gun
› Scissors

Flower Bud

1   Roll a small ball of foil and use a glue gun to attach it to the end of a piece of floral wire.

2   Cut a rectangle from the flower-coloured crêpe paper long enough to wrap around the ball and about two-thirds as wide, with the fine grain of the crêpe running along the length of the piece.

3   Use your fingers to stretch out the centre of the strip to help it fit neatly around the foil ball. Cover the foil with the crêpe paper, glueing it in place.

4   Cut a rectangle of green crêpe paper as before. Twist the centre of the rectangle to form a bow shape, then fold in half. Stretch the centre of the folded paper to form a cup shape. Repeat to make a second identical piece.

5   Each green crêpe piece will have two loose ends. Glue the loose ends together on each piece. Glue the green pieces onto opposite sides of the crêpe-covered foil ball, with the glued bottom ends nearest the wire, and squeeze them together to cup the pieces around the ball.

6   Cut two long eye-shaped pieces of green crêpe and glue one on each side of the ball, with half of each piece attached to the ball and covering the join between the two green cups, and half attached to the wire.

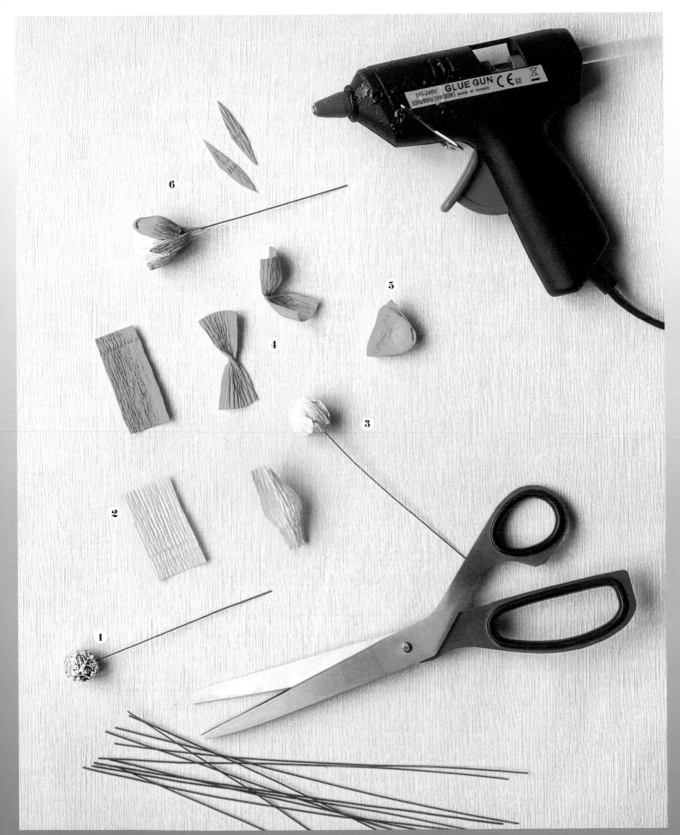

Fringed Flower Centre

MATERIALS
› Flower-coloured Italian crêpe paper
› Green floral wire
› Foil

TOOLS
› Scissors
› Fringing scissors (optional)
› Hot glue gun

1 Cut a rectangle of crêpe paper with the fine grain of the crêpe running across the width of the piece. The width of the rectangle will determine the size of your finished petals and should be long enough to wrap around the wire several times. Use normal or fringing scissors to fringe the paper widthways, leaving a narrow strip uncut along one long edge.

2 If making a flower centre with just a fringe, apply a line of hot glue along the uncut edge of the strip and wrap it around the end of the floral wire.

3 If making a centre with a ball and fringe, make a small flower bud (see page 106, steps 1–3). Glue the fringed strip of crêpe around the base of the bud.

Adding Petals

MATERIALS
› Flower-coloured and green Italian crêpe paper
› Fringed flower centre (see opposite)

TOOLS
› Scissors
› Hot glue gun

1 Cut the required petal shapes from crêpe paper with the grain of the crêpe running vertically down the centre of each petal (use the Flower Petal templates provided on page 182 or make your own; a teardrop shape works well).

2 Place both thumbs in the centre of each petal and stretch the crêpe outwards to form a cup shape.

3 Apply hot glue to the base of the petal and then attach it to the outside of the base of the fringed flower centre, as shown below. Repeat to attach all the petals, overlapping them in a pleasing arrangement.

4 If desired, attach some green crêpe paper leaves around the base of the petals on the back of the flower, as for a flower bud (see page 106, step 6).

Connecting Flower Stems

MATERIALS
› Buds or flowers to be joined
› Green floral tape

TOOLS
› Scissors

1 Wrap the first wire stem with floral tape. When using this, you need to stretch the tape fully to release the glue and allow the tape to stick to itself. Begin at the top (at the base of the bud or flower) and wrap the tape around the stem once, stretching fully and squeezing to encourage the tape to stick to itself, then wind the tape down the stem. Cut the tape when you get to the bottom of the wire.

2 Begin wrapping the next stem as before, starting at the top and winding the tape down to the point where you want the connection to be. At this point, add the first stem and continue wrapping the tape around both stems. Add more stems in the same way as required.

Unstemmed Flowers

MATERIALS

› Heavy paper in several colours

TOOLS

› Scissors
› Pen or pencil
› Fast-drying PVA glue

1 Using the templates (see page 185), cut out a selection of triple petal shapes in different sizes and colours.

2 Place a pen or pencil down the centre of the first petal, as shown below, and wrap the paper around it, squeezing it to curve the petal. Repeat with all the remaining petals.

3 Glue the pieces on top of each other by applying a dot of glue in the centre between each layer, rotating the direction of the petals for a pleasing arrangement.

4 Once the glue has dried, it can help to squeeze the whole flower in your hand, encouraging the petals upwards and together to shape the flower.

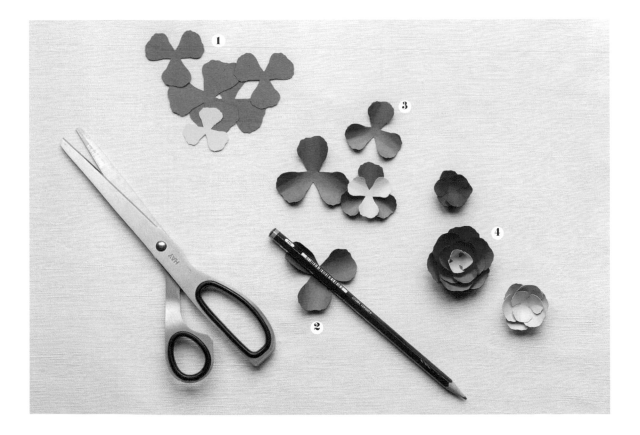

Floral Letter

5

6

4

MATERIALS
To make 1 large letter
› Sheet of A4 paper
› Foamboard (3mm thick, A4 size)
› Green acrylic paint
› Fuchsia pink, pale pink, orange, golden yellow, lemon yellow and green paper (2 sheets each, A4 size)

TOOLS
› Printer (optional)
› Pen or pencil
› Scalpel and cutting mat
› Flat paintbrush
› Scissors
› Fast-drying PVA glue
› Hot glue gun

I love party pieces that translate seamlessly into home decor, and this piece hits just the right note. You can print out the letter on your home computer and even make a giant letter in A0 size. Choose a font that has a bold version to give enough space for the flowers.

1 Draw or print out your desired letter on a spare sheet of A4 paper.

2 Using the paper letter as a template, cut out the shape from foamboard with a scalpel.

3 Paint the foam letter green and allow to dry.

4 Using all of the paper colours except green, make enough unstemmed flowers (see page 111) to cover the foam letter.

5 Using the leaf templates (see page 185), cut out a selection of leaves from green paper and crease them in half lengthways.

6 Check that the letter is dry and then arrange the flowers on top. When you are satisfied with the arrangement, use hot glue to secure the flowers in place.

7 Attach the leaves in the same way, using them to fill the spaces between the flowers.

Flower Power
Party Poppers

MATERIALS
To make 4 poppers
- › Party poppers
  (4 poppers)
- › Black and yellow
  paper (1 sheet
  each, A4 size)
- › Purple tissue paper
  (1 sheet, A4 size)
- › Green floral tape

TOOLS
- › Pen or pencil
- › Scissors
- › Fringing scissors
  (optional)
- › Double-sided tape

If you love confetti and flowers as much as I do, then you need to try these flower poppers now. I like to put a pile in the centre of the table as décor, and then get everyone to pop them later to celebrate.

1 Using the circular end of a party popper as a template (the end opposite the string), trace and cut out circles of black paper.

2 Cut a strip of tissue paper 4cm (1 ½in) wide and long enough to wrap twice around the circumference of the party popper. Use fringing scissors or normal scissors to fringe the strip widthways, cutting about two-thirds of the way through. Wrap the strip around the popper so that the fringing protrudes beyond the end, and secure with double-sided tape.

3 Using the petal template (see page 182), cut out the flower petals from yellow paper.

4 Curl the petals individually by placing a pen or pencil across the top of each petal, as shown opposite. Using your thumb and index finger, hold the pencil and petal together and lightly roll towards the centre.

5 Wrap the petals around the fringing on the party popper, securing with double-sided tape.

6 Wrap floral tape around the rest of the party popper to cover it completely.

7 Use double-sided tape to stick the black circle of paper into the centre of the flower to cover the end of the popper.

Frida Kahlo
Flower Crown

MATERIALS

To make 1 crown
› Foil
› Green floral wire
› White, yellow, fuchsia pink, hot pink, pale pink, purple and green Italian crêpe paper (quantity depends on desired number of flowers)
› Green floral tape

TOOLS

› Scissors
› Hot glue gun
› Fringing scissors (optional)

Inspired by Frida Kahlo's self-portraits, this blossoming floral crown looks abundant with colour. You can fill the crown with flowers for a vibrant, playful look, or arrange them more sparsely and use fewer colours for a softer, more romantic feel. Don't be put off by the quantity of flowers – there are only two types (in varying sizes) and one bud. By playing with size and colour, you can achieve a look that is both impressive and eye-catching.

1 Make a selection of buds, fringe-centred flowers and bud-centred flowers with petal shapes and colours of your choice (see pages 106–109). Wrap all of the stems with floral tape.

2 Measure the circumference of your head where the crown will sit and make a floral wire circle of the same length. If your floral wire is not long enough, simply connect two pieces by twisting the ends together for about 4cm (1½in).

3 Attach the flowers and buds to the crown by laying each stem parallel to the wire crown and wrapping both together with floral tape. Once the flowers are secure, gently turn them to face outwards.

4 When the crown is covered as desired, wrap the entire crown base with floral tape to secure all the flowers together and hide any stray wire or tape.

5 Using the template (see page 182), cut out several pairs of leaves from green crêpe paper. Make sure that the fine grain of the paper runs lengthways along the leaves.

6 Dot a small amount of hot glue into the centre of each pair of leaves, then wrap the leaves around the floral crown to fill any spaces.

Floral Bomb Piñata

MATERIALS

To make 1 piñata
- › Paper lantern
- › Green tissue paper
  (1 pack or roll)
- › Hot pink, purple,
  pale pink and orange
  tissue paper (2 sheets
  each, A2 size)
- › Foil
- › Green floral wire
- › Green floral tape

TOOLS

- › Double-sided tape
- › Scissors
- › Fringing scissors
  (optional)

This beautiful floral bomb can be used as a piñata filled with sweets for birthday parties or hung in the garden as decoration. Covered with tissue paper fringing and lots of flower petals, it looks lovely when hung outdoors with the paper pieces moving in the breeze.

1 Assemble the lantern and use double-sided tape to cover the bottom opening with a piece of green tissue paper.

2 Cut long strips of green tissue paper, about 6cm (2½in) wide. Use fringing scissors or normal scissors to fringe each strip widthways, cutting about halfway through.

3 Starting at the bottom of the lantern, wrap the green fringe around it, as shown opposite, securing with double-sided tape. Cut off excess fringe when a full circle is finished, then add a new layer above it, with the new fringe overlapping the previous layer by about 2cm (¾in). Each layer added should cover the non-fringed portion of the strip below, so that only the fringing shows. Continue until the entire lantern is covered.

4 Make a fringed flower centre (see page 108) with hot pink or pale pink tissue paper and a floral wire stem of about 20cm (8in).

5 Using the template (see page 182), cut out 15 tissue paper petals in any colour except green. Taking stacks of three at a time, pinch and twist them together at the base. Roll them between your thumb and index finger until they are tightly secured.

6 Make five sets of pinched petals, then secure each set around the fringed centre with floral tape. After securing the fifth set of petals, continue wrapping the tape down the stem.

7 Make as many flowers as needed. To attach the flowers, gently lift a small section of the green fringe and puncture the flower stem through the lantern. Thread the stem through until the flower itself sits on the surface of the lantern. Reach inside the lantern to pull on the stem tightly, then secure with tape.

Giant Flower Décor

MATERIALS

To make 1 big flower
› Tissue paper for petals (6 sheets, A2 size)
› Tissue paper for centre (4 sheets, A3 size)
› Green floral wire
› Fishing wire (for hanging)

TOOLS

› Scissors

These giant flowers bring instant sunshine and happiness to any room. Although they look impressive, they are simply two paper pompoms (one big and one small) combined. I love making these as quick decorations and because they are very easy they make a good group project – get a few people to pitch in and you will have a batch in no time.

1 Place the six sheets of tissue paper for the petals together in a stack and pleat into an accordion as if making a pompom (see page 67). Cut triangular tips at each end instead of the usual rounded ones.

2 Repeat this process with the tissue paper for the flower centre, using the same increments for the accordion pleats but this time cutting the usual rounded tips.

3 Open out the pleats on each accordion and place the flower centre stack centrally on top of the petal stack, with the pleats aligned. Refold into a single accordion strip.

4 Secure the centre with floral wire.

5 Fan out both sides of the petal section to create a complete circle. Fluff out the centre section like a pompom.

6 Lightly separate the petal sheets and fluff out a little to give texture.

7 To hang, attach fishing wire to the floral wire at the back of the flower.

Wrapping Paper Origami Lantern

MATERIALS
To make 1 large lantern
› Wrapping paper (3 sheets, A1 size)
› Black/white baker's twine

TOOLS
› Scorer or scalpel
› Ruler
› Sticky tape
› Hole punch
› Scissors
› Double-sided tape

Lanterns are popular in both the origami and home décor worlds, and this version is made using my signature vibrant floral print, which adds interest and contrast to the geometric structure. You can make a mini version of this lantern by using three sheets of a smaller paper size and following the method outlined below.

1 Place the first sheet of paper in front of you with the long edges horizontal. If the paper is single-sided, the front (patterned) side should be facing up. Following the guide on page 187, fold the sheet in half to make a horizontal mountain fold (a fold that points upwards).

2 Make seven equally spaced vertical valley folds (folds that point downwards), dividing the sheet into eight equal columns.

3 Use a scorer or scalpel and a ruler to score diagonal lines as shown on the diagram, using the previous fold lines as guides. Crease these scored lines into mountain folds.

4 Repeat with the remaining two sheets of paper to make three identical pieces.

5 Use sticky tape to join the three sheets together on the back to make one long sheet. Cut off the end column of the strip along the fold as indicated on the diagram.

6 You should now be able to fold the paper inwards (horizontally) from the sides, naturally following the direction of the folds to collapse it into a flat folded piece.

7 Use a hole punch to cut two holes through each layer of the flattened piece. Position the holes as shown in the photograph. You will probably need to do this a few layers at a time, depending on your hole punch.

8 Cut two 50cm (20in) lengths of twine and thread one through each stack of punched holes, then allow the folded paper to open into a round lantern shape. Tie each string securely into a double knot and trim the loose ends.

9 Tuck one end of the lantern under the folds of the other end to complete the spherical shape and secure in place with double-sided tape.

DIFFICULTY

✂ ✂ ✂ ✂ ✂

MATERIALS

To make 1 wreath
› White paper and brown Kraft paper (5 sheets each, A4 size)
› Wooden hoop (20cm/8in diameter)

TOOLS

› Scissors
› All-purpose glue

Every winter my family and I make a different wreath to hang in our home – it's just one of the traditions that gets us into the spirit of the holidays. Half-filled wreaths are all the rage right now and are a contemporary and whimsical take on their traditional fully-filled counterparts.

1 Using the templates (see page 184), cut out a selection of leaves and circles from white and Kraft paper. Cut along the marked lines down the middle of each piece.

2 Take the two sections of paper on either side of the cut and overlap them to give each leaf a slightly cupped shape. Secure with all-purpose glue. Repeat with the circles to make buds.

3 Arrange the shaped foliage onto the wooden hoop piece by piece and secure with glue. For best results, arrange the leaves in clusters fanning outwards, from both the top and underside of the hoop, and hide the centres with multiple buds.

Snowy Gift Wrap with Twig and Tassel Gift Topper

DIFFICULTY

✂ ✂ ✂ ✂ ✂

MATERIALS

To wrap 1 gift and make 1 topper
› Brown Kraft paper
› White acrylic or gouache paint
› Thick wire (1 roll)
› Jute string (1 roll)
› Silver glitter and silver mirror paper
› White tissue paper tassels (2 tassels, 5cm/2in long, see page 67)
› White cotton thread

TOOLS

› Fine paintbrush
› Spare brush or pencil
› Wire cutters
› Scissors
› Double-sided tape
› All-purpose glue

The first time I set eyes on the celebratory papercrafts of Confetti System, I fell in love. This topper made with tassels and glittery bits is a sort of homage to their amazing creations. If you have access to a little branch, feel free to skip steps 2–6 and substitute the real thing.

1 Dip a fine paintbrush in white paint and tap it against something (such as a spare brush or pencil) to speckle the Kraft paper with 'snow'. Allow to dry and then wrap the gift in the snowy paper.

2 To make the topper, cut 30cm (12in) wire, bend in half and twist the two strands together along the whole length.

3 Bend the twisted wire in half. Twist the two halves together to about halfway along, leaving the ends separate to form two 'branches'.

4 To add another branch, cut a 10cm (4in) length of wire and thread it through the twisted loops on the main stem. Bend and twist it for about halfway along its length.

5 Thread the end of the jute string through the loop at the bottom of the main stem and tie a double knot.

6 Wrap the string around the wire, working upwards and covering all the branches except for the top 2–3cm (¾–1¼in) of each branch. Secure the string with a double knot and trim the excess.

7 Cut 5 x 2cm (2 x ¾in) pieces of silver mirror and silver glitter paper; you will need one per branch. Line the underside with double-sided tape.

8 Stick a piece of paper onto the end of each branch. Fold the paper over at an angle to give an irregular geometric shape. Trim off excess paper that is showing white.

9 Attach one or two tassels to the twig topper with white cotton thread to complete.

Tassel Christmas Crackers

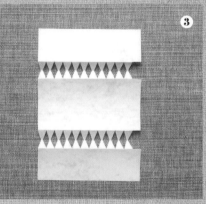

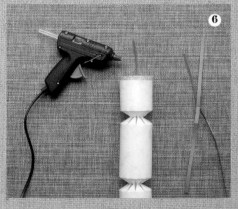

MATERIALS

To make 1 cracker

› Patterned heavy paper (1 sheet, A4 size)
› Silver glitter paper (2 strips, 1 x 15cm/ ⅜ x 6in)
› Cracker snap
› Silver/white baker's twine
› White tissue paper tassel (5cm/2in long, see page 67)
› Sweets, gifts and messages (to fit inside cracker)

TOOLS

› Scissors
› Cardboard kitchen roll tube (optional)
› Double-sided tape
› Hot glue gun

Learn how to make your own version of this holiday staple. Christmas crackers are deceptively simple to make and can add heaps of personality to your festive tablescape. Fill them up with personalized gifts and goodies.

1 Place the patterned paper in front of you with the long edges vertical. Using the picture as a guide, fold the paper.

2 Fold the bottom section upwards and cut out the marked triangles, using the cutting template (see page 186) as a guide.

3 Fold the top section downwards and cut out the marked triangles.

4 With the pattern on the outside, roll the paper into a tube and secure with double-sided tape. You can use a kitchen roll tube to help if you wish; carefully slide it out of the paper tube when you are finished.

5 Use double-sided tape to decorate each end of the cracker with a strip of silver glitter paper.

6 Insert a cracker snap through the cracker body and glue it in place at one end with hot glue.

7 Tie the tassel onto a length of string and then tie this around the perforated section at the end of the cracker with the glued-down cracker snap.

8 Fill the open end of the cracker with toys, sweets and messages, then tie that end closed with string only.

9 Glue down the loose end of the cracker snap on the inside of the cracker.

Snowball
Lantern

✂ ✂ ✂ ✂ ✂

MATERIALS

To make 1 lantern
› Paper doilies (100 pieces, 9cm/3½in diameter)
› Paper lantern

TOOLS
› All-purpose glue
› Double-sided tape (optional)

This lantern takes a little while to complete, but it is not difficult to make at all. I love the pretty, snowy look of the white doily decoration, but mixed pastel shades would be equally charming.

1 Fold each doily into quarters and crease. Unfold so that the creases make a cross on the horizontal and vertical axes.

2 Flip the doily over and rotate 45 degrees. Crease by folding in half from top to bottom. Unfold and flip it back over.

3 The doily should now have two larger sections at the top and bottom. Push the left and right sides of the doily in towards the centre, in the direction of the horizontal fold, to make a little cone shape.

4 Press the folded doily flat with the tip at the bottom. Fold the tip up and apply glue to it.

5 Open up the paper lantern and line the closed doilies all around the lantern and secure in place with glue or double-sided tape. When the lantern is covered, fluff open the doilies.

Doily Garlands

DIFFICULTY
✂ ✂ ✂ ✂ ✂

MATERIALS
To make multiple garlands
› Paper doilies (9cm/ 3½in diameter)
› White cotton thread or fishing wire

TOOLS
› Needle
› Scissors
› All-purpose glue (optional)

A simpler variation of the Snowball Lantern (see page 131), these lovely garlands are perfect for quick and easy decorations. Arrange the folded doilies closer together for a more romantic look, and experiment with different ways of hanging to give interest to your decorations.

1 Prepare the doilies as for the Snowball Lantern (see page 131, steps 1–3). The quantity depends on the length of garland you wish to make.

2 Using a needle and doubled length of thread or fishing wire, sew through the centre of the doilies, tying a double knot to secure each one in place. If the knots don't hold the doilies in place, add a small dot of glue.

DIFFICULTY

✂ ✂ ✂ ✂ ✂

MATERIAL

To make 1 teabag
› Silver mirror card or white card (10cm/4in square)
› Teabag on string

TOOLS

› Scissors
› Glue stick

A good cup of tea really can fix everything. Try serving this with breakfast in bed to give the treat an extra-special touch. Oh, and bonus points for writing a cute message on your hearts.

1 Using the template (see page 184), cut out two hearts from silver mirror card or white card. Cut along the marked slot line.

2 Cut off the branded tag on the teabag. Glue the heart tabs together, with the end of the teabag string sandwiched in between.

3 Pour boiling water into your mug and put the teabag inside. Slide the heart tag onto the rim of the cup to make it sit up straight, then serve.

I Want to Liquorice You Chair Streamers

DIFFICULTY

✄ ✄ ✄ ✄ ✄

MATERIALS

To make multiple streamers

› Hot pink, pale pink, yellow and black crêpe streamers (1 roll each)

TOOLS

› Scissors
› Double-sided tape

I love reinventing childhood crafts in a contemporary way. At school I made paper garlands like these to decorate the noticeboard at the back of the classroom, and I remember that the stock coloured paper made them distinctly the domain of 'children's crafts'. Switching the paper stock to transparent streamers and using a more considered and controlled colour palette definitely gives them the update they needed. These chair streamers scream fun without being too bright or unrefined.

1 Cut two 50cm (20in) long pieces of streamer in the colours of your choice.

2 Place one strip (strip 1) horizontally, with one end in front of you. Place the other strip (strip 2) vertically on top, so that the end aligns with the top of the horizontal strip. Secure with double-sided tape.

3 With one hand holding down where the two pieces intersect, use the other hand to fold strip 1 over horizontally so that it is now on top of strip 2. Press down and crease.

4 With one hand holding down where the two pieces intersect, use the other hand to fold strip 2 over vertically so that it is now on top of strip 1. Press down and crease.

5 Continue folding the streamers in this way, alternating directions, until you reach the end. Secure the two ends with double-sided tape as before.

6 Make as many streamers as required and tape one end of each streamer to the back of the chair.

Sticky Notes Wall

MATERIALS
To make 1 backdrop
› Square sticky notes in several colours
› Gold contact paper (1 roll)

TOOLS
› Scissors

This wall decoration is probably the easiest backdrop to make on the planet. It requires no prepping and is 100 per cent fun, so put on some music and get sticking.

1 Arrange the sticky notes on your display wall about 2cm (¾in) apart.

2 Cut out a few squares of gold contact paper the same size as the sticky notes and cover a few of the notes in gold for a special accent.

Sprinkles Confetti Balloons

✂ ✂ ✂ ✂ ✂

MATERIALS
To fill 1 balloon
› Confetti (store-bought or hand-cut, see page 150)
› Clear balloon

TOOLS
› Funnel (optional)
› Balloon pump

These confetti balloons are simple but genius at the same time. The static makes some of the confetti stick to the wall of the balloon while the rest floats around inside. You can buy confetti balloon kits from more high-end party stores, but why not make your own at a fraction of the price? Confetti can be made for next to nothing, and you will have control over the colours and shapes too.

1 Spread out the confetti and touch as many pieces as possible with your fingers so that the static will make them stick to the inside wall of the balloon.

2 Use a funnel (or ask a friend) to hold the balloon open while you push a handful of confetti inside.

3 Inflate the balloon with a balloon pump (or with your mouth if you feel brave).

Sparkling Candles Birthday Cards

2

3

4

DIFFICULTY

✂ ✂ ✂ ✂ ✂

MATERIALS
To make 1 card
> Neon-coloured washi tape
> Coloured card (A5 size, folded into A6)
> Gold glitter

TOOLS
> Old newspaper or plastic
> Scissors
> PVA glue with nozzle
> Spray mount

Neon tape is one of my absolute favourite things. This card design is so easy to make that you will be finished in 10 minutes. It's also the perfect project to have up your sleeve if you haven't had time to pop to the shops to buy a card.

1 Line your work surface with old newspaper or plastic. Lay the card in front of you with the folded edge at the top.

2 Cut 5–6 strips of washi tape, about 4–5cm (1½–2in) long. Arrange them on the card, as shown opposite, leaving some space at the top for the candle flames.

3 Apply dots of glue just above the top of each candle. Sprinkle with plenty of gold glitter and shake off the excess.

4 With one stroke only, apply Spray Mount across the top of the card above the candles. Take a pinch of glitter and sprinkle it loosely across the sprayed area to create sparkling flames. Allow to dry overnight.

Ice Lolly Party Invitations

DIFFICULTY

MATERIALS

To make 8 invitations
› White card (2 sheets, A4 size)
› Blue, yellow and green gouache or watercolour paints
› Lolly sticks (8 pieces)

TOOLS

› Scissors
› Old newspaper or plastic
› Flat paintbrush
› Paint dish
› Double-sided tape or PVA glue

I am a big fan of special-shaped invitations, and these ice lolly ones are full of fun. If you are feeling adventurous, try using different kinds of paint, such as glitter paint or even metallic paint.

1 Using the lolly template (see page 185), cut out a total of 16 ice lolly shapes from white card.

2 Line your work area with old newspaper or plastic. Paint 8 of the lollies, one colour at a time, as shown opposite, washing the brush clean between each colour. Leave the other side white. Allow to dry.

3 Use double-sided tape or PVA glue to attach each painted card to a lolly stick.

4 Using a black brush pen, write your party message onto one side of the remaining white card lolly shapes. Tape or glue them onto the reverse of the painted lollies, sandwiching the sticks in between.

MATERIALS
To make 6 cards
› White paper (1 sheet, A4 size)
› Iridescent and purple card (1 sheet each, A4 size)

TOOLS
› Scissors
› Masking tape
› Scalpel and cutting mat
› Ruler
› PVA glue with nozzle

This card is beautiful because of its simplicity and precious miniature size. The finished card will fit into a mini C7 envelope.

1 Photocopy six copies of the gemstone template on page 184. Each copy will be used to make one gem.

2 For each gem, cut the white paper, iridescent card and purple card into a solid gem shape, as pictured.

3 Lay a gemstone template on top of the white paper gem, taping it in place with a small piece of masking tape. Use a scalpel and ruler to cut out all the inner triangles marked on the template, cutting through both the template and the white paper beneath.

4 Glue the iridescent gem on top of the purple gem.

5 Using the nozzle on the PVA glue, lightly line the underside of the white gem cutout. Position it carefully on top of the iridescent card and press together.

Iridescent Geometric Bowls

✂ ✂ ✂ ✂ ✂

MATERIALS

To make 1 bowl
> › Thin card (3 squares of equal size)

These geometric bowls require no glue and minimal cutting (if you have square paper to hand, then no cutting at all). Hurray! There are many versions of these bowls out there, but I love this pastel and iridescent combination.

1 Fold each square of card in half diagonally to make a triangle.

2 With the long folded edge of each triangle at the bottom, fold the top point down to touch the bottom edge. Crease and unfold.

3 Fold the bottom right and bottom left corners up to the top point, as shown opposite. Crease and unfold.

4 Referring to the photograph as a guide, connect the three triangles by slotting them together in a row.

5 Bring the two ends together and slot them into each other to form the rim of the bowl. The right-angled points of the triangles will overlap to form the base.

All Kinds
of Confetti

Need confetti? First decide which type, because different kinds of confetti suit different situations. Confetti is easy to make but takes a little bit of time and repetition. However, store-bought packets can be expensive so making your own can save you lots of money, especially if you need a lot of it for throwing around.

Types of confetti

- Lightweight confetti is usually made from tissue paper so that it will fall slowly. It tends not to fall in clumps, so it is perfect for confetti balloons (see page 140) and confetti gift wrap (see page 70) as well as for photographing. Its floatiness gives it a soft, romantic feel.

- Heavyweight confetti is made from more substantial paper including metallics. You can also use ready-made items such as sequins. It is perfect for decorations and scattering across tables.

Making confetti

- Punched confetti is really easy to make. Craft stores sell punches in lots of different shapes, including circles, squares, hearts and even butterflies, so you can have lots of fun punching. You can also make small paper confetti using a standard hole punch.

- Shredded/rough-cut confetti can be made using a shredder or fringing scissors. Fringe the paper lengthways and then cut across the fringing to make small strips of confetti. One of my favourite tricks is to repurpose a metallic party curtain, roughly cut into sections.

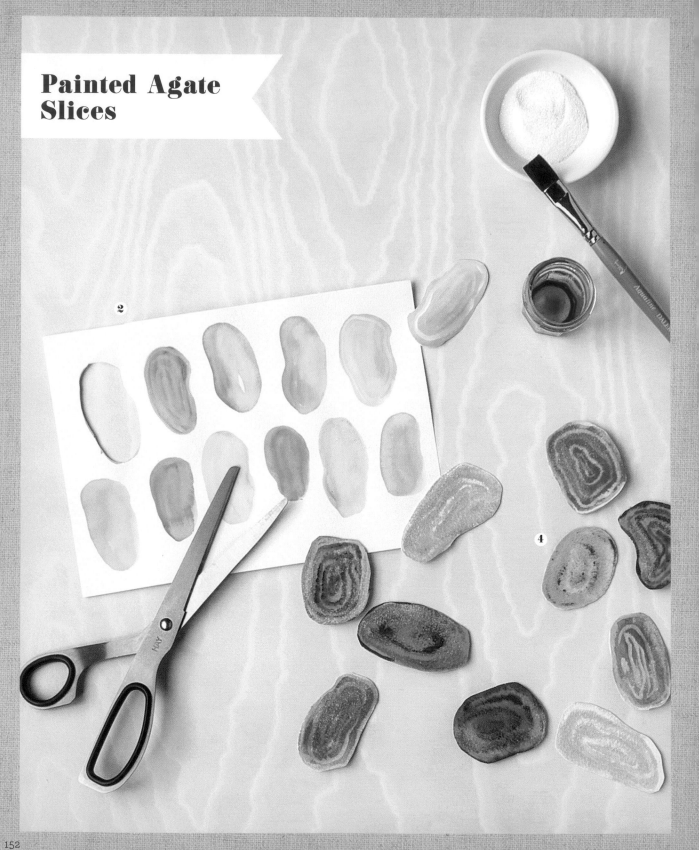

Painted Agate Slices

DIFFICULTY
✂ ✂ ✂ ✂ ✂

MATERIALS
To make 10–12 slices
› Coloured and white
  water-based paints
› White gouache paint
› White watercolour
  card (1 sheet, A4 size)
› Fine white glitter

TOOLS
› Paint dish
› Flat paintbrush
› Fine paintbrush
› Scissors
› PVA glue

Using heavyweight card for this project is essential so that it will not curl up or buckle when the watery paint is applied. Painting the slices takes a bit of experimentation, so try lots of different shapes and sizes until you get a result you like.

1 Mix a coloured wash in the paint dish, starting with a small blob of paint and adding water to dilute until satisfied.

2 Using a flat brush, paint irregular ovals onto the watercolour card for the agate shapes.

3 While still wet, use a fine brush and white gouache paint to make a pattern of rings on the agate shapes, as shown opposite. Allow to dry.

4 Cut out the shapes and apply a thin layer of PVA glue to each slice. To make them shimmer, sprinkle glitter on top and shake off the excess.

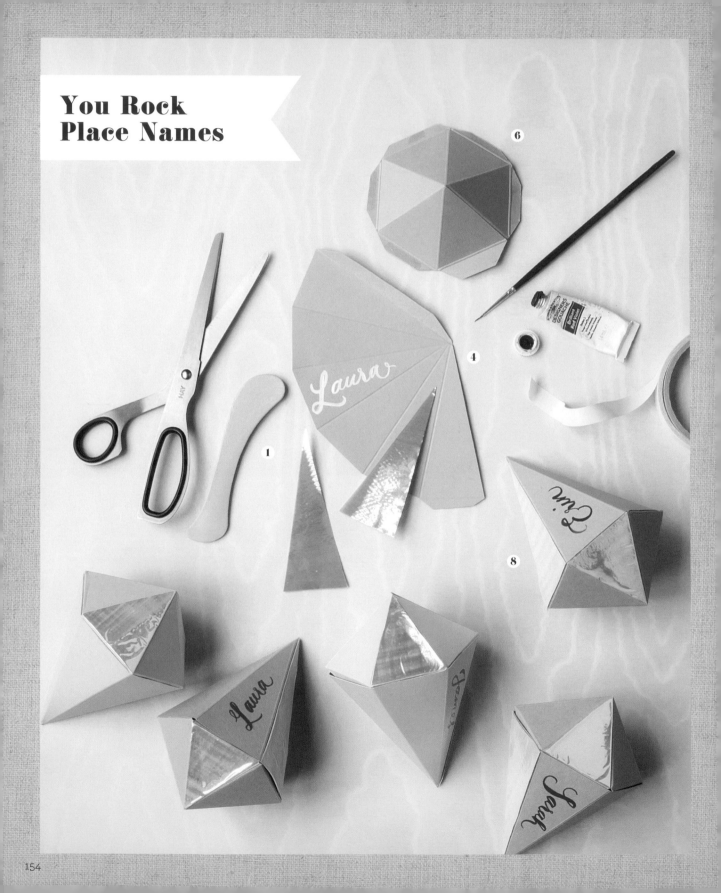

MATERIALS

To make 1 gem

> Pale purple or blue card (1 sheet, A4 size)
> Iridescent card or paper (1 sheet, A6 size)
> White or purple gouache paint

TOOLS

> Scissors
> Scorer
> Ruler
> Fine paintbrush
> Double-sided tape
> PVA glue

This project is everything I love about modern craft: it looks clean and contemporary and hits the right trends. The construction of the gem does take a little patience, but the result is well worth your time and it feels really satisfying when you finish.

1 Using the templates (see page 183), cut out the top and bottom sections of the gem from coloured card and the two triangle segments from iridescent card.

2 Using a scorer and ruler, score the lines marked on the templates onto both pieces of coloured card.

3 Paint the name of the guest or recipient on one of the segments on the bottom section of card.

4 Assemble the bottom of the gem by folding along all of the scored lines. Apply a strip of double-sided tape along tab A and press it into place to form an angular cone shape.

5 Repeat this process with tab B to assemble the top cone of the gem.

6 Line all of the remaining tabs with double-sided tape and join the top and bottom cones together.

7 Using PVA glue, stick the iridescent triangles onto a top and bottom segment of the gem.

Mermaid Scales Backdrop

MATERIALS

› Purple, blue and iridescent paper (for scales)
› Blue paper (for backdrop)

TOOLS

› Large-circle hole punch (about 6.5cm/ 2½in)
› Double-sided tape

I love making backdrops that can be kept as big works of art, and this mermaid background is exactly that. When the scales catch the light, the iridescent paper makes such pretty reflections. If the size of this looks a little too intimidating, why not start with a smaller version as a piece of artwork?

1 Punch out circles of paper in various colours.

2 Starting at the bottom of the backdrop sheet of paper, apply strips of double-sided tape in horizontal rows spaced 6.5cm (2½in) apart.

3 Unpeel the bottom strip of tape and arrange the circles on it side by side, filling the entire strip. Position the circles so that they are centred on the tape, with the top of the circle just below but not touching the strip of tape above. It is important to arrange the circles neatly so that no tape will be visible when the backdrop is complete.

4 Unpeel the next strip of tape and attach the next row of circles, tucking them under the ones in the row below. Continue until the entire backdrop is filled.

158

DIFFICULTY
✂ ✂ ✂ ✂ ✂

MATERIALS
To make 3 bottles
› Black card (1 sheet, A4 size)
› White gouache paint
› Gold glitter
› Gold ribbon (3mm/⅛in wide)

TOOLS
› Scissors
› Fine paintbrush
› PVA glue
› Double-sided tape or all-purpose glue
› White or light-coloured gel pen

My love of glitter knows no bounds and I try to sneak it into anything I am working on. These bubbly cards are the perfect excuse to use gold glitter. You will need long envelopes to fit the shape of the cards. Ask at your stationery shop for DL envelopes (the standard long envelopes used for documents) and your champagne bottle will fit in there perfectly.

1 Using the template (see page 184), cut out the champagne bottles from black card.

2 Paint your message on the front of each bottle with white gouache.

3 Apply a little PVA glue to the tip of the bottles on the front of the card and lightly spread with your fingertip.

4 Pour glitter over the top, shake off the excess and allow to dry.

5 Cut several strands of gold ribbon, each about 7cm (2¾in) long, and use another piece of ribbon to tie the strands together at one end to form a tassel. Make two more tassels.

6 Using double-sided tape or all-purpose glue, attach the knotted end of the tassels to the tip of each bottle on the reverse of the card.

7 Use a white or light-coloured gel pen to write your 'thank you' message on the reverse.

DIFFICULTY

✂ ✂ ✂ ✂ ✂

MATERIALS

› Envelopes for
lining, plus a spare
› Plain paper
(1 large sheet)
› Patterned wrapping
paper (1 large sheet)

TOOLS

› Scissors
› Pencil
› Glue stick

These easy envelope liners will jazz up any plain-looking note. All you need is a bit of spare wrapping paper and an envelope and your post will instantly look 100 per cent more impressive.

1 Take a spare envelope of the same shape and size as the one you wish to line. Carefully open up all the flaps and lay it flat.

2 Cut off the side and bottom flaps. Then trim off 1 cm ($^3/_8$in) around the whole piece, including the top flap. This will be your template for the liner.

3 Place the template onto the wrapping paper, draw around it and then cut out.

4 Insert the liner into a new envelope and glue in place, positioning it as shown opposite.

Chic Personal Stationery

MATERIALS

To make 8 cards in each of 3 designs
› White card (3 sheets, A4 size)
› Pink water-based paint
› Hot pink envelopes (24 pieces, C7 size)

TOOLS

› Lipstick
› Masking tape (optional)
› Hairspray
› Scissors or scalpel and cutting mat
› Ruler
› Fine paintbrush
› Black brush marker

I am such an advocate of personal stationery. It represents the sender and, being blank, can be used for different occasions. In our world of instant messaging and social media, personal stationery can seem a little redundant, but consider this: have you ever bought a gift and just wanted to write a quick note? If you had a boxful of your own handmade stationery, this would never be a problem again.

1 To make the lip-printed card, apply lipstick to your own lips and use them to print the pattern onto a sheet of white card. For best results, use masking tape to stick the card to a wall at eye level. Keeping your lips relaxed and making a small O shape, press them onto the card and roll your head to one side and then the other. Reapply lipstick between each stamp. For variation, try two colours of lipstick.

2 Once the entire card is evenly printed, spray it with hairspray to lock in the colour and prevent smudging.

3 Cut each sheet of card (one lip-printed and two blank) into eighths (A7 size).

4 Paint 'XOXO' on half the blank cards, as shown opposite. Use a black marker to draw Breton stripes on the remaining ones.

5 Write your message on the reverse of the card and pop into a hot pink envelope.

Baguette
Wrappers

BONJOUR!

BONJOUR!

BONJOUR!

MATERIALS
To make 8 wrappers
› Wrapping paper
  in two designs
  (1 sheet each,
  minimum A4 size)
› White card
  (1 sheet, A4 size)
› Baguettes
  (8 small rolls)
› Jute string

TOOLS
› Scissors
› Black brush marker
› Double-sided tape

Sometimes the simplest ideas are the best. These baguette wrappers are so quick to make you won't believe it. All you need is some wrapping paper and string and you're good to go.

1 Cut the wrapping paper into 20 x 5cm (8 x 2in) strips.

2 Cut rectangles of white card, about 6 x 5cm (2½ x 2in). Place the cards in front of you with the short edges horizontal and use a black marker to write messages, starting at the top edge.

3 Place a white card on top of a baguette roll and wrap the paper strip around them twice, with the message peeping up above the wrapper. Secure the end of the wrapper with double-sided tape.

4 Wrap with jute string and tie a bow at the front.

Pop-up Lips Tent Cards

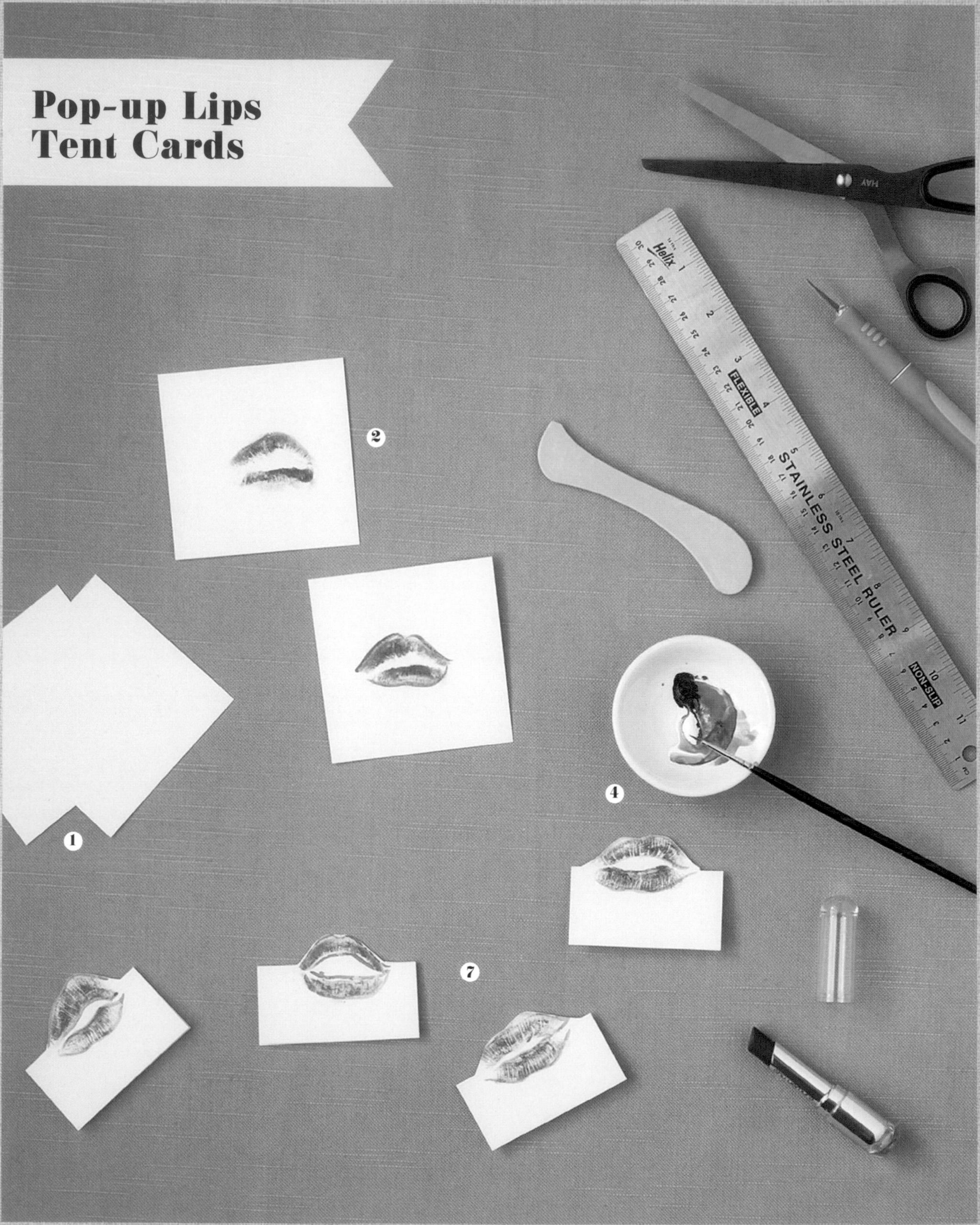

DIFFICULTY
✂ ✂ ✂ ✂ ✂

MATERIALS
To make 12 cards
› White card (1 sheet, A3 size)
› Pink water-based paint

TOOLS
› Scissors
› Lipstick
› Hairspray
› Fine paintbrush
› Scorer
› Ruler
› Scalpel and cutting mat

I love using lips as a motif because they feel so chic and timeless. This pop-up version of a tent card will add a fun pop of pink to your table setting.

1 Cut out twelve 9cm (3½in) squares of white card.

2 Apply lipstick to your own lips and use them to make a lip print on the centre of each card. For best results, keep your lips relaxed and make a small O shape. Press them onto the card and roll your head to one side and then the other. Reapply lipstick between each stamp.

3 Spray the printed lips with hairspray to prevent smudging.

4 Outline the lips with pink paint to give definition.

5 Using a scorer and ruler, score across the middle of the card on either side of the lip print.

6 Use a scalpel to cut around the top half of the lips, from the end of one scored line to the other.

7 Fold the card in half so that the lip print pops up.

4

2

6

168

MATERIALS
To make 1 box
› Marble-patterned
  thin card (1 sheet,
  A3 size)
› Pale blue thin card
  (1 sheet, A4 size)
› Gold glitter

TOOLS
› Scissors
› Scorer
› Ruler
› Double-sided tape
› PVA glue with nozzle

I'm a sucker for lovely packaging, so this macaron box is one of my favourite projects. To make one box, all you need is 2 sheets of card, one A3 size and the other A4, plus a sprinkling of glitter to add on top.

1   Using the templates (see pages 184 and 185), cut out the body of the box from marble-patterned card and the sleeve from blue card.

2   Using a scorer and ruler, score the lines marked on the templates onto both pieces of card.

3   Apply a strip of double-sided tape to all of the tabs marked on the templates.

4   Apply little dots of PVA glue to the front section of the box sleeve. Pour gold glitter on top, shake off the excess and allow to dry.

5   Assemble the body of the box by first folding along all the scored lines and then securing with double-side tape. Assemble the sleeve in the same way.

6   Carefully push the body of the box inside the sleeve.

Floral Print
Food Cones

MATERIALS

To make 2 cones
- › Patterned paper
  (1 sheet, A4 size)
- › Gold glitter tape

TOOLS
- › Scissors
- › Double-sided tape

Somehow, presenting food in a cone makes it tastier – in my opinion, anyway, although I admit that I'm a sucker for street food and things to eat on the go. To get the right look for these cones, choose a patterned wrapping paper with a retro feel, or scan a bit of retro floral fabric and print it out in colour.

1 Place the paper in front of you with the long edges horizontal. Fold down the top right corner so that the right edge aligns with the bottom edge of the sheet and make a crease.

2 Cut off the rectangle exposed along the left edge and discard. Unfold the paper; it should be a perfect square. Cut along the diagonal crease line to make two triangles.

3 To make each cone, place a triangle in front of you with the long edge at the bottom and the right-angled corner at the top. If the paper is patterned on one side only, the patterned side should be underneath.

4 Fold the right-hand point over to align with the left-hand point and make a tiny crease at the bottom to mark the centre. Unfold.

5 Apply a strip of double-sided tape along the bottom right-hand edge of the triangle on the underside of the paper, from the right-hand point as far as the central crease.

6 Place a finger on the left side of the central crease. Take the right-hand point of the triangle in your other hand and twist it around, aligning the point with the left half of the top right-angled corner to create a cone shape. Press down on the taped edge to secure.

7 Wrap the remaining paper on the left-hand side around the cone and attach with double-sided tape.

8 Apply glitter tape around the top of the cone, sticking it around the inside first and then folding it over to the outside. You may need to apply a layer of double-sided tape between the glitter tape and cone if the glitter tape is not sufficiently sticky.

Retro Print Cutlery Holders

4

6

DIFFICULTY

✂ ✂ ✂ ✂ ✂

MATERIALS

To make 1 holder
› Double-sided patterned paper (1 sheet, A4 size)
› Brown Kraft paper (1 sheet, A5 size)
› Cutlery and condiments

TOOLS

› Ruler
› Double-sided tape
› Scissors

Ever been to a party with a lovely spread of nibbles but found it tricky to hold the plate, napkin and various bits of cutlery? This little folded holder contains all the essentials for your guests, who will thank you for being so thoughtful.

1   Place the patterned paper in front of you with the long edges vertical. Measure 17cm (6¾in) from the top edge and fold the paper downwards. Unfold.

2   Measure 6cm (2½in) from the bottom edge and fold the paper upwards (don't unfold this time). Refold the top of the paper down again. Turn the paper over so that the folded 'pocket' is uppermost and at the bottom, then set aside.

3   Place the Kraft paper in front of you with the long edges horizontal. Measure 4cm (1½in) from the top edge and fold the paper downwards to the back of the sheet.

4   Insert the Kraft paper into the patterned paper pocket, with the folded edge of the Kraft paper at the top. Push the Kraft paper right to the base of the pocket and align the left and right edges.

5   Measure 7cm (2¾in) from the right edge and fold backwards.

6   Measure 5mm (¼in) from the left edge and fold backwards, then measure a further 4.5cm (1¾in) from the left edge and fold backwards.

7   Turn the cutlery holder over so the back is facing you. Use double-sided tape to secure the double-folded edge on top of the single-folded edge, and to attach the front and back layers at the top of the holder together.

8   Trim the top edge to neaten if necessary. Tuck your cutlery and condiments inside.

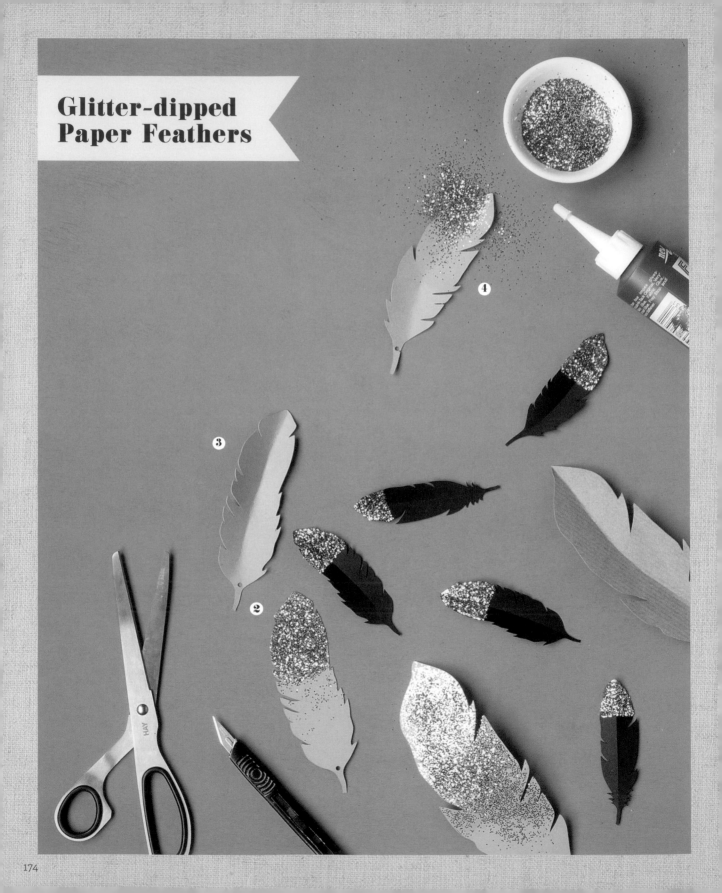

MATERIALS

To make multiple
feathers

› Thin card in
  black, brown or
  another colour
› Gold glitter
› Coffee stirrers
  (for feather stirrers)
› String (for garland)

TOOLS

› Scissors
› Hole punch
  (for garland)
› Scorer or scalpel
› PVA glue (for
  stirrers)

Glittered feathers are all kinds of wonderful. They are
charmingly retro and beautiful in equal measure. Channel
a bit of boho chic and work them into your party decor.

1 Using the templates at your desired size (see page 185),
cut out the required feather shapes from thin card.

2 If making a garland, punch a hole near the quill end of
each feather.

3 Use a scorer or scalpel to score down the centre of
each feather from tip to quill. Gently crease along the
scored line.

4 Apply PVA glue to the tip of the feathers (or where
desired). Cover with glitter and tap off the excess.

5 To make drink stirrers, glue a coffee stirrer onto the back
of each feather.

6 To make a feather garland, thread a length of string
through the punched holes.

Oops-a-Daisy Chain Choker

MATERIALS

To make 1 choker
- › Mustard yellow Italian crêpe paper (8mm x 25cm/ ¼ x 10in)
- › White Italian crêpe paper (20 x 5cm/ 8 x 2in)
- › Green floral wire (50cm/20in)
- › Gold ribbon (3mm/ ⅛in wide)

TOOLS

- › Scissors
- › Flat-nosed pliers (2 pairs)
- › Hot glue gun

A choker is a lovely alternative to a flower crown and is set to make a comeback. The daisies take a little patience to craft, but practice makes perfect.

1 Use scissors to fringe the yellow crêpe paper widthways, cutting about two-thirds through. Cut the strip into eight equal sections. Using the template (see page 183), cut 64 petals from white crêpe paper. Stretch each one in a curve.

2 Gently bend the floral wire back 2cm (¾in) at the end to form a U shape. Hold the open end of the loop with one pair of pliers and twist the loop around with another pair.

3 Just after the twisted loop, use pliers to bend the wire up at a 90-degree angle. About 8mm (¼in) further along, bend the wire tightly back on itself. Bend the wire horizontal again after another 8mm (¼in) to form the first 'stalk'.

4 After a gap of 3cm (1¼in), repeat to make a matching stalk. Continue until you have eight stalks, all pointing in the same direction. After the last stalk, measure 4cm (1½in) of wire and trim off the excess. Make a secure loop to match the one at the other end of the wire.

5 Use a glue gun to attach the end of a fringed yellow crêpe paper strip to the first stalk, with the fringed edge sticking up above the stalk. Tightly wrap the fringed paper around the stalk, glueing as you go to secure in place. Repeat with the remaining stalks.

6 Now attach the white petals, using eight per flower. Apply a dot of glue to the base of the first petal and stick it over the yellow paper, touching the base of the stalk. Attach the next three petals in a compass point formation. Apply four more petals in the gaps between the first four. Complete the remaining flowers in the same way.

7 Cut two equal lengths of ribbon. Thread one through the first wire loop and glue the end in a loop around the wire loop. Repeat at the other end.

8 Gently curve the wire into a round shape to create the choker.

Cupcake
Anemones

MATERIALS

To make 1 flower

- › Paper cupcake holders (2 holders)
- › Black crêpe paper (15 x 3cm/6 x 1¼in)
- › White gouache or acrylic paint
- › Small ball of tin foil

TOOLS

- › Scissors
- › Glue stick
- › Flat paintbrush
- › PVA glue

Paper cupcake holders have lovely ridges that make very pretty petals when cut up. White ones are found at most supermarkets, but you can also purchase colourful (non-patterned) ones to vary your flower colours.

1 Cut each cupcake holder into eighths and round off the top two corners of each piece to make a petal.

2 Use a glue stick to join four petals together at the pointed tips. Repeat until you have four sets of four petals.

3 Stack the four sets of petals together in a nice arrangement and join them at the centre using the glue stick.

4 To make the flower centre, cut a 10 x 3cm (4 x 1¼in) strip of black crêpe paper. Apply white paint to one side, leaving about 5mm (¼in) unpainted along one long edge. Allow to dry.

5 Wrap the remaining crêpe paper around the ball of foil. Secure the loose ends of the paper with PVA glue.

6 Use scissors to fringe the strip, starting at the unpainted edge and cutting about two-thirds of the way through. Wrap the fringe around the ball of foil, with the unpainted edge outwards. Secure with PVA glue and allow to dry.

7 Use PVA glue to stick the fringed flower centre into the centre of the cupcake petals.

Scallop-edged
Stationery

✄ ✄ ✄ ✄ ✄

MATERIALS

To make 2 folded
cards with envelopes
and 2 tags

> › Black card (1 sheet,
>   A4 size, for cards;
>   1 sheet, A7 size,
>   for tags)
> › Grey square-flap
>   envelopes (2 pieces,
>   C6 size)
> › Gold glitter
> › Black/white
>   baker's twine

TOOLS

> › Scissors
> › Scorer or scalpel
> › Ruler
> › Hole punch
> › PVA glue

Scallop edging has been having a big moment recently in the fashion world as a quiet, understated alternative to lace trimmings, which can sometimes feel a bit elaborate. This lovely feminine trend, translated to stationery, makes for very chic post indeed.

1   Cut the A4 sheet of black card in half widthways. Using the templates (see pages 186–187), cut out the scalloped edging around the cards and cut out the gift tags from the A7 sheet of black card.

2   Use the template to cut a scalloped edge along the envelope flaps.

3   Using a scorer or scalpel and ruler, score across the centre of each card and fold.

4   Use a hole punch to cut out a hole in the top of the gift tags.

5   Apply a line of PVA glue along each scalloped edge and around the gift tag holes. Cover with glitter and then tap off the excess.

6   Thread a length of twine through each gift tag hole.

Templates

Doughnuts (About You) Toppers

Replicate templates at 100%

Frosty Snowflake Gift Toppers

Replicate template at 200% for larger snowflake, or 50% for smaller snowflake.

Twinkling Stars Advent Calendar

Replicate template at 200%

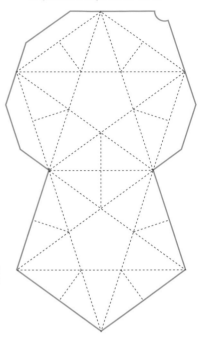

Astronaut Messages

Replicate template at 200%

Rocket point

Flower Power Party Poppers

Replicate template at 200%

Floral Bomb Piñata

Replicate template at 100%

x15 per flower

Flower Petals

Replicate template at 100%

You will need:

A x 5 per flower
B x 3 per flower (green)
C x 6 per small daisy flower
D x 16 per large daisy flower

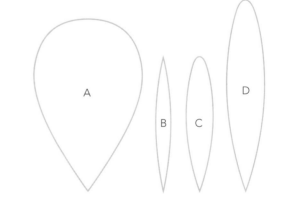

Frida Kahlo Flower Crown

Replicate template at 100%

You will need:
x 10 approx per crown (green)

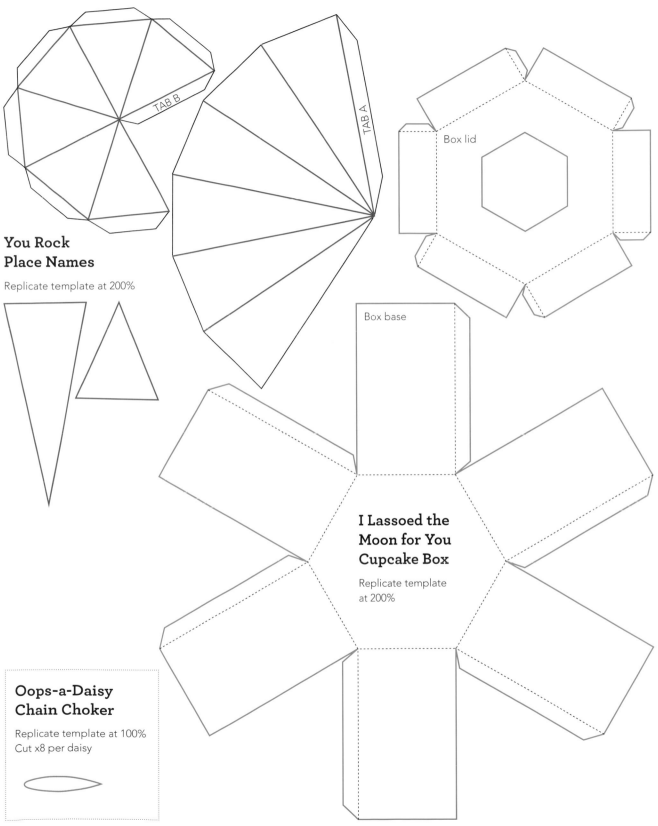

**You Rock
Place Names**

Replicate template at 200%

TAB B

TAB A

Box lid

Box base

**I Lassoed the
Moon for You
Cupcake Box**

Replicate template
at 200%

**Oops-a-Daisy
Chain Choker**

Replicate template at 100%
Cut x8 per daisy

Foliage Wreath

Replicate templates at 100%

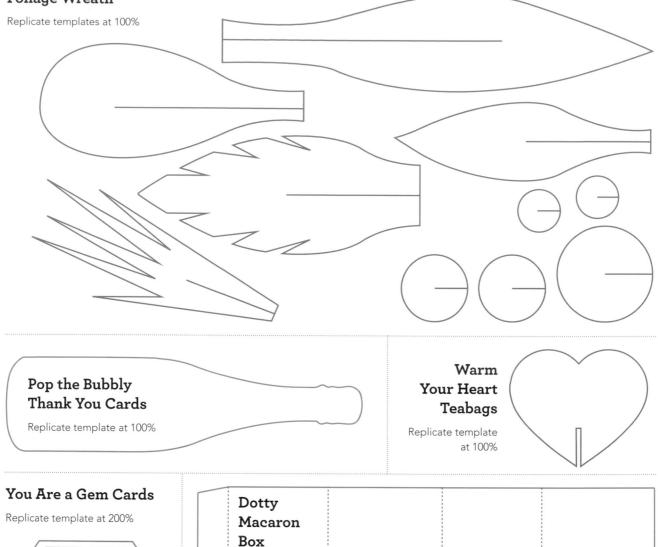

Pop the Bubbly
Thank You Cards

Replicate template at 100%

Warm
Your Heart
Teabags

Replicate template
at 100%

You Are a Gem Cards

Replicate template at 200%

Dotty
Macaron
Box

Replicate
template
at 200%

Box sleeve

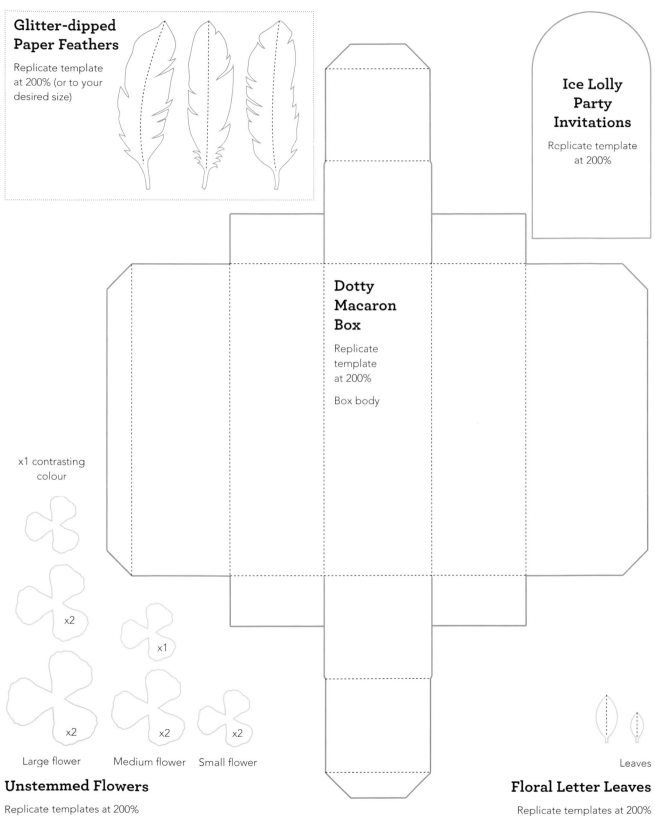

Glitter-dipped Paper Feathers

Replicate template at 200% (or to your desired size)

Ice Lolly Party Invitations

Replicate template at 200%

Dotty Macaron Box

Replicate template at 200%

Box body

x1 contrasting colour

x2

x1

x2

x2

x2

Large flower

Medium flower

Small flower

Unstemmed Flowers

Replicate templates at 200%

Leaves

Floral Letter Leaves

Replicate templates at 200%

Ice Cream Cone Messages

Replicate template at 100%

Cone

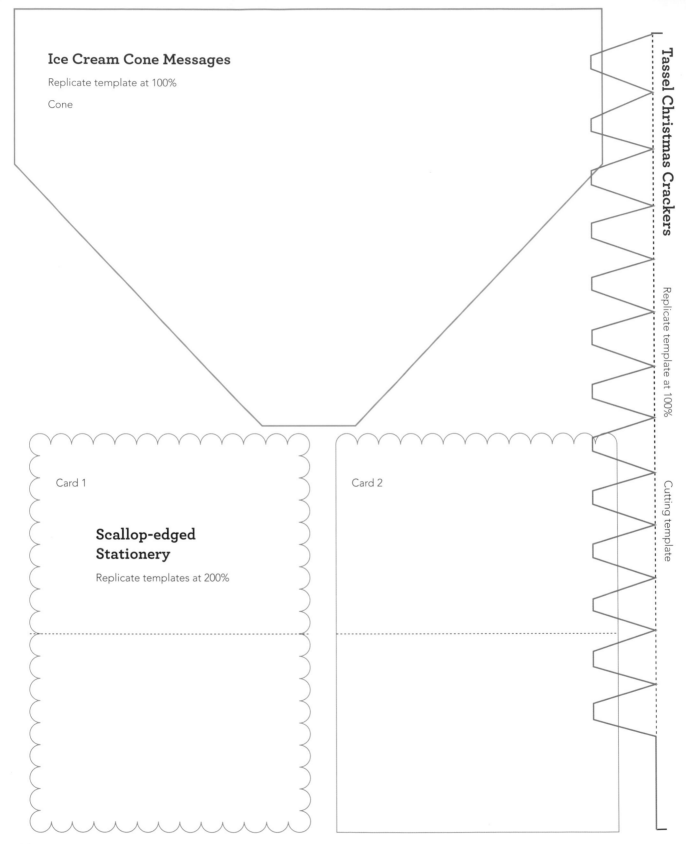

Tassel Christmas Crackers

Replicate template at 100%

Cutting template

Card 1

Scallop-edged Stationery

Replicate templates at 200%

Card 2

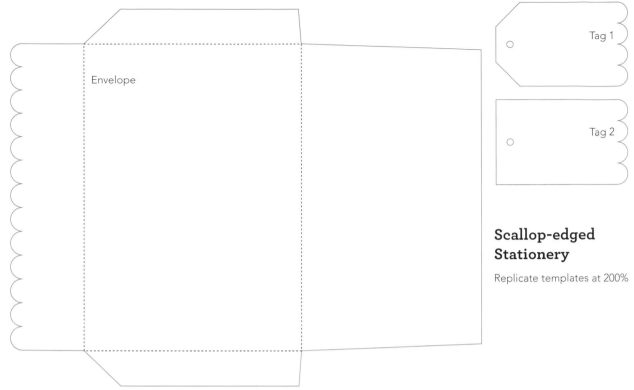

Envelope

Tag 1

Tag 2

Scallop-edged Stationery

Replicate templates at 200%

Guides

Wrapping Paper Origami Lantern

Step 1

Step 2

Step 3

Step 4

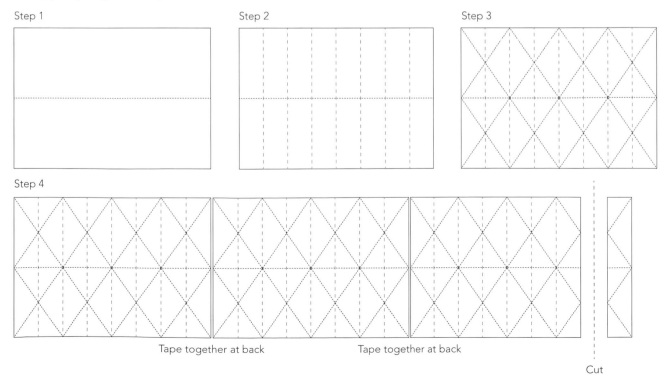

Tape together at back

Tape together at back

Cut

Secret Love Messages

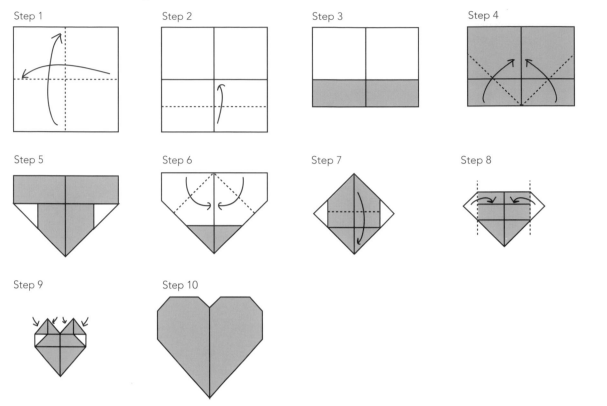

Step 1

Step 2

Step 3

Step 4

Step 5

Step 6

Step 7

Step 8

Step 9

Step 10

Tie the Knot Announcements

A NOTE ABOUT PAPER SIZES

Many of the projects in this book use readily available A-sized sheets of paper. If you do not have A-sized papers, use the chart below to measure and cut your own sheets.

A0

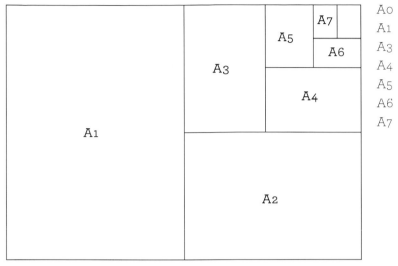

A0	841 x 1189mm (33 x 46¾in)
A1	594 x 841mm (23½ x 33in)
A3	297 x 420mm (11¾ x 16½in)
A4	210 x 297mm (8¼ x 11¾in)
A5	148 x 210mm (5¾ x 8¼in)
A6	105 x 148mm (4 x 5¾in)
A7	74 x 105mm (3 x 4in)

A NOTE ON ENVELOPE SIZES

The C series of envelopes (and the DL) are designed to fit sheets of A-sized paper. Size conversions are below.

p95
C6: 11.4 x 16.2 cm /4½ x 6½ in

p147
C7: 8.1 x 11.4cm/3⅛ x 4½in

p159
DL: 22 x 11cm /8⅝ x 4¼ in

p163
C7: 8.1 x 11.4cm/3⅛ x 4½in

p181
C6: 11.4 x 16.2cm/4½ x 6½ in

PARTY RESOURCES

Planning a party? Here is my little black book of my favourite party people and suppliers, should you need a little help along the way.

FLOWERS
Blue Sky Flowers
www.blueskyflowers.co.uk
Run by Liz Inigo Jones, Blue Sky Flowers is a renowned wedding florist based in London, providing high quality bespoke displays from their studio at New Covent Garden Market to couples and clients all over the South East. They also provide beautiful flowers for private parties and events in and around London. Consultations by appointment.

Bloomfield of London
www.newcoventgardenmarket.com
Bloomfield Wholesale Florist are a family run business based at London's iconic New Covent Garden Market. They import an incredibly diverse selection of flowers daily from across the globe and are constantly awed by the magic created by the florists they work with. They have a wealth of knowledge about the flowers they provide and are happy to help in sourcing particular items to fit their client's requirements.

HOMEWARE
Dot Com Gift Shop
www.dotcomgiftshop.com
Since 2005, dotcomgiftshop has been creating gorgeous and original gifts and accessories for the home - exclusively designed or lovingly chosen by their in-house design team. With a talented team of British designers, they've created an evolving range for her, him and the kids – as well as curated collections of everything you could possibly need for any special occasion. So whether you're planning a country wedding or a glorious garden party, a retro picnic, or a pirates and princesses jamboree – Dotcomgiftshop will have the answer.

Bombay Duck
www.bombayduck.com
The unmistakable Bombay Duck style embraces the colourful, imaginative and pretty by discovering the fabulous in the everyday. Designed in London, the signature look confidently mixes bright exotic colours, playful patterns, vintage and modern designs with detailed finishing and an element of surprise. Collections include fashion accessories, homewares, gifts, kids and baby.

LUXURY CHOCOLATES
Whimsical Cake Company
www.thewhimsicalcakecompany.co.uk
The Whimsical Cake Company are passionate about creating edible works of art for special occasions, creating chocolates, cookies, candy, dessert tables and bespoke wedding cakes. Their aim is to create things that are fresh, full of flavour and pleasing to the eye, creating edible treats for life's occasions.

PARTYWARE
Peach Blossom
www.peachblossom.co.uk
Vibrant and creative party shop Peach Blossom is your first stop for pretty, stylish and modern party decorations. Founder Alyssa Williamson is on a mission to give parties a good shake up, so she has carefully selected beautiful decorations from around the world which she hopes will not only excite you but also inspire you to make your celebrations extraordinary.

CAKES
Pretty Gorgeous Cakes
www.prettygorgeouscakecompany.co.uk
Pretty Gorgeous Cake Company is one of the UK's leading cake designers specialising in wedding and celebration cakes. Established in 2009 by Cynthia Stroud, the cake designers have won multiple national awards including best Wedding Cake designers in London and South East and have been the official cake suppliers to the Brit Awards Afterparty for the last 6 years. The company based in Hertford and London covers London, Hertfordshire, Edsex, Beds, Cambridgeshire and Surrey.

HIRE
Bo Boutique Props Hire
www.boboutique.co.uk
Bo Boutique are Floral Design and Styling experts who curate events worldwide, with a strong emphasis on the finer detail. With a background in fine art and floristry, natural materials play a huge part in their transcendent and signature style. In addition to event curation is the Bo Hire range of luxury antique props and contemporary tableware, for hire throughout the UK.

Glimmer & Threads
www.glimmerandthreads.com
Glimmer & Threads is a London based sequin linen hire, event styling and planning boutique business. With over 10 years in the event business we come with a wealth of experience whether you are looking to add a little sparkle to your next dinner party, add a lot of glamour to your wedding day or plan your upcoming birthday soiree, they are here to help!

PARTY STYLIST
Laura Burkitt
www.lauraburkitt.com
Laura Burkitt is a freelance lifestyle and event stylist with over 10 years experience in the industry. After graduating from Central St.Martins, she went on to work for numerous publications, including Condé Nast Brides where she spent four successful years as Lifestyle Stylist. Laura works with commercial clients including The Gordon Ramsay Group and Goodwood House, as well as styling private weddings and events.

PAPER
GFSmith
www.gfsmith.com
For over 130 years, G. F. Smith has been obsessed with the simple beauty of paper. With head offices in Hull and London, their collection of beautifully curated papers sourced from around the globe has never been as comprehensive or more ideally suited to meet the demands of the modern creative as it is today and remains without equal.

PAPER CREDITS

G. F. Smith
www.gfsmith.com

We would like to thank G. F. Smith for generously providing their beautiful and functional papers used in the projects throughout this book. Below are the papers we have used from their selection, so that you will be able to source the same colours and quality of papers:

p. 78–79 Doughnuts (About You) Toppers
Candy Pink, 120gsm

p. 80–81 Tie the Knot Announcements
Bright White, 270gsm

p. 82–83 You Float My Boat Place Names
Bright White, 270gsm

p. 86–87 Ahoy Flag Stirrers
Cool Blue, 270gsm

p. 90–91 Ice Cream Cone Messages
Bright White, 270gsm

p. 98–99 Frosty Snowflake Gift Toppers
Bright White, 270gsm

p. 100–101 Twinkling Stars Advent Calendar
marlmarque 200gsm

p. 104–105 I Lassoed the Moon for You Cupcake Box
marlmarque 200gsm

p. 112–113 Floral Letter
Fuchsia Pink, Candy Pink, Mandarin, Factory Yellow, Forest; all 120gsm

p. 114–115 Flower Power Party Poppers
Ebony, Factory Yellow; both 175gsm

p. 124–125 Foliage Wreath
Bright White, 175gsm

p. 128–129 Tassel Christmas Crackers
marlmarque 200gsm

p. 142–143 Sparkling Candles Birthday Cards
Tuquoise, Fuchsia Pink, Emerald, Mandarin; all 270gsm

p. 144–145 Ice Lolly Party Invitations
Bright White, 270gsm

p. 146–147 You are a Gem Cards
Lavender, 270gsm

p. 148–149 Iridescent Geometric Bowls
Azure blue, 135gsm

p. 154–155 You Rock Place Names
Lavender, Azure Blue; both 270gsm

p. 156–157 Mermaid Scales Backdrop
Lavender, Azure Blue; both 120gsm

p. 158–159 Pop the Bubbly Thank You Cards
Ebony, 270gsm

p. 162–163 Chic Personal Stationery
Bright White, 270gsm

p. 166–167 Pop-up Lips Tent Cards
Bright White, 270gsm

p. 168–169 Dotty Macaron Box
marlmarque 200gsm, Azure Blue, 270gsm

p. 174–175 Glitter-dipped Paper Feathers
Stone, Ebony; both 175gsm

p. 180–181 Scallop Edged Stationery
Ebony, Real Grey; both 270gsm

These papers are available to purchase at www.colorplanpapers.com

Acknowledgements

I'm astounded by the undeserved support graciously given to me throughout this process, for which I am forever humbled and grateful.

My heartfelt thanks to Pavilion, for making this book possible – Ione and Krissy my editors and Michelle my designer. To Laura my stylist and Charlotte and Lana my photographers, your professionalism, input and enthusiasm made this project such a joy to complete. To the rest of the book team who has done a stellar job of support and administration – thank you.

My love and thanks to Ben, for your endless patience, encouragement, and tireless belief in me; I shall always remember our one fateful conversation outside the Tate Britain and hold it close to my heart.

To my mum, you taught me from a young age to pursue my dreams; and my dad, your passion for and belief in your work inspires and motivates me to do the same everyday. I love you both.

Thanks to Daryl, for tolerating my glitter and craft messes since childhood, and letting me turn your flat into Paper Parties HQ.

To the rest of my family and friends who supported me in this adventure: thank you!

And finally, to everyone who has followed my work, tried my DIYs, sent me photos of what you've made – you make it so very worthwhile and my heart is so full because I'm able to do what I love.

About BerinMade

BerinMade is a stationery and lifestyle brand based in London, UK. With a penchant for all things print and paper, we design and produce custom stationery such as invitations for weddings and events, as well as other cool goodies like greeting cards, notebooks, and wrapping paper, sold all over the world. Our signature love of fun patterns, bold colours and boundless imagination is the heartbeat of the company; and we aim to spread joy through paper, one project at a time.

Sponsors and Friends

We would like to express our gratitude to G. F. Smith, for providing their stunning paper range for the crafts in this book (more details on page 191), and to Adejoke, my fantastic paper rep, for sending me copious amounts of paper to make it all possible.

Our thanks go to our fabulous partners and friends, for the use of their amazing and sometimes delicious products in the Lookbook:

Oliver Bonas
Bombay Duck
Benugo UK
Cole & Son
Whimsical Cake Company
Keep It Sweet
Peach Blossom
Talking Tables
Dot Com Gift Shop
Blue Sky Flowers
Pretty Gorgeous Cake Company
Bo Boutique Props Hire
Glimmer & Threads

Credits

Lookbook Photographer: Charlotte Tolhurst
Creative Consultant and Stylist: Laura Burkitt
Tutorials Photographer: Lana Louw
Craft Assistant: Sarah Louise Matthews
Photoshoot Assistant: Susannah Crook
Make Up and Hair: Kylie McMichael

First published in the United Kingdom in 2017 by
Pavilion
43 Great Ormond Street
London
WC1N 3HZ

ISBN 978-1-911216-25-4

A CIP catalogue record for this book is available from the British Library.

10 9 8 7 6 5 4 3 2 1

Repro by Colourdepth
Printed and bound by 1010 Printing International Ltd, China

This book can be ordered direct from the publisher at www.pavilionbooks.com